The Roman Republic

A Captivating Guide to the Rise and Fall of the Roman Republic, SPQR and Roman Politicians Such as Julius Caesar and Cicero

© **Copyright 2018**

All rights Reserved. No part of this book may be reproduced in any form without permission in writing from the author. Reviewers may quote brief passages in reviews.

Disclaimer: No part of this publication may be reproduced or transmitted in any form or by any means, mechanical or electronic, including photocopying or recording, or by any information storage and retrieval system, or transmitted by email without permission in writing from the publisher.

While all attempts have been made to verify the information provided in this publication, neither the author nor the publisher assumes any responsibility for errors, omissions or contrary interpretations of the subject matter herein.

This book is for entertainment purposes only. The views expressed are those of the author alone, and should not be taken as expert instruction or commands. The reader is responsible for his or her own actions.

Adherence to all applicable laws and regulations, including international, federal, state and local laws governing professional licensing, business practices, advertising and all other aspects of doing business in the US, Canada, UK or any other jurisdiction is the sole responsibility of the purchaser or reader.

Neither the author nor the publisher assumes any responsibility or liability whatsoever on the behalf of the purchaser or reader of these materials. Any perceived slight of any individual or organization is purely unintentional.

Free Bonus from Captivating History (Available for a Limited time)

Hi History Lovers!

Now you have a chance to join our exclusive history list so you can get your first history ebook for free as well as discounts and a potential to get more history books for free! Simply visit the link below to join.

Captivatinghistory.com/ebook

Also, make sure to follow us on:
Twitter: @Captivhistory
Facebook: Captivating History:@captivatinghistory

Contents

INTRODUCTION – THE ROMAN REPUBLIC: AN EMPIRE BEFORE THE EMPIRE 1
    Why is the Roman Republic that important? 1
    The Republic of Plato or… 2
    Chronology 3

CHAPTER 1 – THE PAST THAT MADE IT POSSIBLE: THE FOUNDATION OF ROME BETWEEN MYTH AND HISTORY 5
    A Tale of Rape, Murder, and Abduction – the Legend of Romulus and the Foundation of Rome 6
    Act One: Divine Rape and Failed Infanticide 7
    Act Two: Family Reunion and Fratricide 8
    Act Three: The Asylum 9
    A Poetry Interlude 9
    Epilogue 10

CHAPTER 2 – DOWN WITH THE KINGS: THE PAST THAT MADE IT HAPPEN 11
    A Patricide: The Death of Servius Tullius, the Last Honorable King of Rome 12
    The Arrogant King and the Death of Roman Monarchy 14
    The Romans vs. the Kings 15

CHAPTER 3 – EARLY REPUBLIC 16
    The Dawn of Liberty 16
    The Clash that Defined Rome: The Conflict of Orders and the Twelve Tables 17
    Everyday Lives of Ordinary Romans in the Republic 20
    Women in Rome 22
    Public Life 23

CHAPTER 4 – MILITARY ACHIEVEMENTS OF EARLY REPUBLIC: TAKING ITALY 25
    The Gauls 26
    The Samnites 27

THE GREEKS 29

CHAPTER 5 – MIDDLE REPUBLIC: THE PUNIC WARS AND MEDITERRANEAN DOMINANCE 31

THE PHOENICIANS (*PUNICI*) AND CARTHAGE 31
THE FIRST PUNIC WAR 32
ROME'S AMBITIONS 33
FIGHTING AT SEA 33
THE SECOND PUNIC WAR: HANNIBAL AND SCIPIO 35
HANNIBAL'S TRIUMPHS; THE BATTLE AT CANNAE 36
THE CHANGES IN ROMAN TACTICS 37
ROME'S NEW BLOOD: SCIPIO AFRICANUS 38
THE AFTERMATH OF THE SECOND PUNIC WAR 39
THE END OF CARTHAGE 39

CHAPTER 6 – THE MILITARY VS. CULTURAL DOMINANCE: THE ROMAN CIVILIZATION MEETS THE GREEK WORLD 41

GREECE AFTER ALEXANDER THE GREAT 42
THE ROMANS COME TO GREEK TERRITORY 42
ROME, MACEDON AND THE FREEDOM OF GREECE 43
GRAECO-ROMAN CULTURE AND THE TENSION 45

CHAPTER 7 – LIMITLESS POWER AND THE BEGINNING OF THE END: THE LATE REPUBLIC 47

THE ORIGIN OF CRISIS..48
THE ANGRY CROWD 48
A NEW CLASS: THE EQUESTRIANS..49
THE GRACCHI 49
MARIUS, THE FIRST WARLORD 51
THE WAR AGAINST ALLIES: THE SOCIAL WAR 52
SULLA'S MARCH ON ROME 52

CHAPTER 8 – THE AGE OF THE GENERALS: POMPEIUS, CRASSUS, AND CAESAR 53

GNAEUS POMPEIUS 53
MARCUS LICINIUS CRASSUS 54
JULIUS CAESAR 54
THE FIRST TRIUMVIRATE (60 BC) 55
CAESAR AND THE GAULS 55

CHAPTER 9 – SENATUS POPULUS-QUE ROMANUS (SPQR) AND ITS DOWNFALL 57

CICERO AGAINST CATILINE: THE STORY THAT ENCAPSULATES 63 BC ROME 58

CHAPTER 10 – THE RISE AND FALL OF JULIUS CAESAR AND THE END OF THE ROMAN REPUBLIC 61

CAESAR VERSUS POMPEY 61
CROSSING THE RUBICON 62

    A Romantic Digression: Caesar and Cleopatra 63
    Triumph at Rome 65
    Mark Antony or Octavian 66
    The End of the Republic (44–43 BC) 67

CONCLUSION **68**

TIMELINE **70**

REFERENCES **94**

Introduction – The Roman Republic: An Empire before the Empire

When we think of ancient Rome, the first notion that comes to mind is the one of the empire, followed by the image of a mighty emperor, his legions, colossal buildings, and the Gladiators (or the rhetoric and poetry, depending on your preferences). Some may recall the image of a "unified" Europe under a single sovereign – the emperor of Rome. However, Rome did not become remarkable at this considerably late phase. In fact, many historians see the history of Rome under the Emperors as a long, gradual decline. Centuries behind, many Romans shared this view. They talked and wrote about their glorious past obsessively – but who wouldn't? Their past made the empire not only possible; it made it real. It was during the Republic that Rome gained an empire. Most of the achievements that the first emperor of Rome, Octavian Augustus, claimed to have completed were, in fact, earned during the Roman Republic.[i]

Why is the Roman Republic that important?

The Roman Republic shaped the unique culture of Greco-Roman fusion as we know it from art, literature, rhetoric, philosophy, architecture, and law. The rise of the Republic was the rise of the city of Rome – once a small, ordinary Italian settlement that had become a metropolis with a million inhabitants who dominated the Mediterranean. The notion of Rome's republican politics influenced great minds from Plutarch, Tacitus, and Shakespeare, to the philosophers of the European Enlightenment, and the American Founding Fathers. It is still relevant today. Another fusion – the one of the classic republican political system and the culture of spectacle and performance – still defines our world at every possible level. The image of Roman legions served as a basis for the clone and Stormtrooper legions of the fictitious Galactic Empire. The assassination of Julius Caesar, on the other hand, has given the pattern and excuse for the killing of tyrants in the real world, ever since.[ii]

The history of ancient Rome is the history of western civilization and a significant part of the history of the world. The Roman culture is the foundation of our own culture and politics. Our ideas of liberty and citizenship, as well as the terminology of modern politics, including senators and dictators, have been defined and thoroughly used in antiquity. The way we laugh at ourselves and the world around us, too. The world's finest satire-writers were ancient Romans. They invented entertainment through fear as well. Even though the Romans did not write horror novels (if they did, those novels would undoubtedly be amazing just as their works in other forms), they watched horror in the arena. The outcomes of their bloody spectacles with the Gladiators were unpredictable. But let's not go too far. In this book, we'll have a close look at the beginning of Roman civilization, the foundation of the city and the Senate, the expansion of the Roman Republic, its glory, and its end.

The Republic of Plato or...

You'll recognize many elements of present-day democracy, including its ugly side, blatant political marketing, reputation management, populism, intrigue, and the occasional murder. Indeed, the Romans used to kill each other way too often for such civilized folks, but they justified those assassinations eloquently and convincingly. Thanks to the abundance of written documents from the Romans themselves, we can delve deeply into their motives and ambitions, and discover the real stories behind most controversial events that involved treasons, spy-mistresses, and murders.

The Roman Republic had two faces. One of them was impeccably clean, with white togas,[iii] high rhetoric, the advanced constitution of the city-state, and an elevated sense of virtue, justice, and pride. The other face was characterized by the lust for power, conspiracies, and obscure wealthy individuals who ruled from the shadow, letting others do the politics in public. Some Roman politicians loved to say they were living in the ideal state – the Republic of Plato, while in fact, Rome was instead the *faex* (feces) of Romulus, as Cicero joked in a private letter.[iv]

The culture of ancient, republican Rome was one of openness and diversity from the very beginning. The sense of identity and belonging was based on the idea of citizenship, not the origin. Highly educated people discussed the nature of freedom and the problems of sex, just as we do today. But this cosmopolitan city also had a dark side. The glorious political constitution turned out to be rotten inside. There were also slavery, filth, and illnesses everywhere. Death was just around the corner on the streets, just as it was in the Senate. Eventually, the Roman Republic fell entirely by itself.

The end of the Roman Republic was also a new beginning, as it resulted in the foundation of a new era known as the Roman Empire. This will be the subject of the book two in this series.

Chronology

You can find a precise timeline at the end of the book. For now, let's just sketch the history of the Roman Republic in a few short sentences. The mythical city foundation took place in 753 BC. The authentic Roman republican political system was developed by the late fourth century BC. The third century was a period of bloodshed, struggle, and uncertainty, marked by the Punic Wars. The second century was an antithesis to the third; Rome's legions almost effortlessly defeated Hellenistic towns and kingdoms throughout the Mediterranean. Rome had become huge and immensely powerful. And corrupt, soon after. The first century BC is one of the most exciting periods in world history and, especially, in the history of Ancient Rome. New turmoil was caused from inside. Political fights, corruption, lawlessness, and civil war characterized this period. Few generals controlled the political scene and held all the power, while the traditional institutions became useless. That was the age of Cicero and Catiline, Julius Caesar and, at the very end, the Emperor Octavian Augustus, with whom this period (and this book) ends and the next begins.

Chapter 1 – The Past that Made It Possible: The Foundation of Rome between Myth and History

This history of the Roman Republic begins with a mythical tale. The Emperor Octavian Augustus had employed various notable cultural workers, the most important of which was certainly Virgil, who wrote an account of Troyan hero Aeneas, depicting him as the founder of Rome. Augustus needed to create a new national myth and establish a different—nicer and cleaner—sort of cultural identity. However, the first, authentic story the ancient Romans could resonate with was the one that follows.

There are a couple of good reasons, to begin with, the story of Romulus and Remus. Firstly, the Romans themselves included the tale in their histories. They did not do so because they were naïve. They were, in fact, just as skeptical about the notion of a wolf feeding two human infants as we are. They told the story over and over because it was important. It shed – and it still does – a special light to the very sense of Romanness. It tells a lot about whom the Romans were and how they saw themselves. Another reason is that, simply, we've got no choice. We've got no proof the story is either false or true. Any archeological evidence had been eaten up back in antiquity, thanks to a constant, intense process of urbanization.

Finally, in a broader sense of the term, history does include the knowledge of myths and legends. Surprisingly, it looks like the Romans did not think much about the origin of the world, as their central myth is not about the creation of the Universe (aside from the tendency to make Rome the center of it) but of the foundation of the city. Therefore, we'll take a closer look at this fascinating story.

A Tale of Rape, Murder, and Abduction – the Legend of Romulus and the Foundation of Rome

Myths are weird. A commonsense logic doesn't help to process them. All myths have strange and illogical elements, but this one is particularly bizarre. The story of Rome is full of unheroic elements – let's add throwing newborn babies to the list in the heading. Its protagonists belong to the lowermost level of society, and include murderers, possibly prostitutes (Livy[v] points out to the similarity between the word wolf and a colloquial expression used for a prostitute, and wonders whether it was the former who took and breastfeed the baby brothers), outlaws and runaways from all around the peninsula and beyond.

There are many different versions of the story, and a couple of them had been written down in ancient times. While Cicero avoided writing about supernatural elements (he only mentioned the odd detail of the god Mars as the father of the twins, and moved on, focused on geographical assets of the place Romulus had chosen for the city). Other writers, such as Ovid, made fun criticizing the way Romulus solved the problem of establishing the first Roman marriages and families. The most detailed account of Romulus's life and the early history of Rome – and the one we will stick with – is the one of Livy.

Act One: Divine Rape and Failed Infanticide

So, this is the story. Once upon the time, there was a little kingdom called Alba Longa. Its king, Numitor, was thrown out from the throne by his brother, Amulius. To make sure there would be no throne pretenders from his brother's line, Amulius forced Numitor's daughter, Rhea Silvia, to become a virgin priestess. However, she was not quite a virgin; soon it became clear she was pregnant. Now, there are two explanations for her pregnancy. Rhea Silvia claimed the god Mars raped her. Many ancient writers believed the claim and wrote about a *disembodied phallus coming from the flames of the sacred fire.*[vi] Livy, on the other hand, was thinking what we are thinking. The god of war was just a convenient invention to conceal an entirely human affair. Anyway, the priestess gave birth to two boys, and Amulius quickly ordered his men to throw the newborns into the river Tiber to drown. The servants could not bring themselves to complete the task, so they left the babies on the shore. A *lupa* (either a female wolf or, as Livy assumed, a prostitute) found them and offered them her nurturing breasts. Finally, a compassionate shepherd took them in.

The Capitoline She-Wolf was an icon of Rome since antiquity. The age and origin of the figures is a subject of controversy. The Lupa was long thought to be an Etruscan work of the 5th century BC, with the twins added in the late 15th century AD, but radiocarbon and thermoluminescence dating has found that it was possibly manufactured in the 13th century AD.

Act Two: Family Reunion and Fratricide

When they grew up, the legendary brothers accidentally met their grandfather Numitor, helped him to reclaim the throne of Alba Longa, and left to establish their own city. Unfortunately, they could not agree on the precise location where they should find the city. Out of the famous seven hills, Romulus picked the Palatine, whereas Remus opted for Aventine. Romulus paid no attention to his brother's wishes and started constructing the defenses around his preferred site. Remus insultingly jumped over them, and Romulus killed him, shouting afterward: "So perish anyone else who shall leap over my walls."[vii]

Act Three: The Asylum

The city had been built with Romulus as the sole ruler. There was just one problem left – Rome had very few citizens. Romulus came up with an innovative idea and declared Rome an asylum. He encouraged the outcasts of the rest of Italy to join him. The city was soon filled with convicted criminals, runaway slaves, and other immigrants. But there were no women, and without women, there was no future. Romulus made a new cunning plan. He invited the neighboring peoples to a festival. The Sabines and the Latines, whole families, came in great numbers. In the middle of the proceedings, Romulus signaled his men to capture the young women among the guests and to take them away as their wives. There is no consensus over how many accidental brides were kidnaped (the estimates vary from 30 to 683), yet the very first Roman marriages started off with mass abduction and rape.

A Poetry Interlude

"O Romulus, you are the only one who has ever known how to reward his soldiers;

for such pay, I would willingly enroll myself beneath your banners."

—Ovid, *Ars Amatoria*[viii]

While "serious" Roman thinkers, such as Cicero, Livy and Sallust tried their best to either justify or condemn Romulus's decisions, less serious ones were openly ironical. The poet Publius Ovidius Naso – widely known in our century as Ovid, the author of *Metamorphoses* – included the famous legend in his most controversial work, *Ars Amatoria* (*The Art of Love*). Ovid refers to the rape of Sabine women to point out that the theatre has always been a good place to meet girls. It was Romulus who "first mingled the cares of love with public games." We'll never know for sure whether those (and many similar) lines compelled Augustus to banish the poet from Rome, or the *Ars Amatoria* was just an excuse for the expulsion, hiding some political secret. Augustus certainly had a lot to hide, and Ovid's links with the emperor's grandchildren made the poet very unfortunate. His exile has been revoked in AD 2017.[ix] We can certainly agree it was slightly too late.

Epilogue

The captured Sabine women – now wives and mothers – bravely stopped the war that was initiated after their abduction. According to the legend, the young wives entered the battlefield and begged both sides – their Sabine fathers and Roman husbands – to stop fighting. They did not want to become orphans or widows, and they said they would rather die themselves. Their mediation worked and resulted in peace. Rome became a shared Roman-Sabine town, under the joint rule of Romulus and Titus Tatius, the Sabine king. Tatius was murdered a couple of years later, the same way as many other Roman rulers and politicians were yet to die: violently, during a riot. The pattern of fratricide and civil conflict was established early in the Roman history.

Chapter 2 – Down with the Kings: The Past that Made It Happen

According to Livy, Rome had been under the rule of 'kings' – seven of them – for two and a half centuries. Romulus disappeared mysteriously during a storm. Either he had ascended to the heavens as the god Quirinus[x], or this was another political murder, yet a primitive monarchy had already been established.

We are still somewhere between myth and history. The primary sources for this period are part fables – part historiography, but they are still very important for the history of Rome. Many details about the kings do not make much sense. Their chronology is most obviously problematic; seven kings over the 250 years would mean each of them ruled for more than three decades, on average. That consistent level of longevity is physically impossible. More probably, either the monarchy lasted much shorter than the Romans estimated, or there were more kings in between.

The first of the six kings following Romulus was a Sabine called Numa Pompilius. He was said to be an easygoing individual who conceived most of the Roman religious traditions, including the Vestal Virgins, the title of Pontifex, and even the modern western calendar with all its months. The second monarch (or third if we count from Romulus) was Tullus Hostilius, a notorious warrior responsible for the demolishing of Alba Longa, the ancestral city of many Romans. Next was Ancus Marcius, Numa's grandson. He was both a warrior and a tradition keeper, and the founder of the Rivermouth, Rome's seaport at Ostia. The fourth king after Romulus was Tarquinius Priscus, also known as 'Tarquin the Elder.' Unlike his predecessors on the throne, he was of the Etruscan origin. He expanded the city, established the Roman Forum and the Circus Games, and initiated the work on the great Temple of Jupiter on the Capitol above the Forum. His successor Servius Tullius was a political reformer who devised the Roman census and defined the city by the construction of the Servian Wall.

A Patricide: The Death of Servius Tullius, the Last Honorable King of Rome

Servius Tullius deserves our special attention, for several reasons. He was "the wisest, most fortunate and best of all Rome's kings."[xi] Yet he was the only king whose father's name had been omitted from the list in the Forum. Roman kings had diverse backgrounds: Numa and Titus Tatius were Sabines; Tarquin the Elder came from Etruria and had a Greek (Corinthian) origin. Servius Tullius's case was special. According to the ancient legend, Servius had no father; his mother (who was a servant; hence "Servius") was said to have encountered and was penetrated by a divine, fire-made phallus.[xii] He was in fact either the son of a slave or a war prisoner. His case is yet another example that even at the very beginning of the Roman political order, 'Romans' could come from somewhere else. Even those born very low (including ex-slaves and their sons) were allowed a chance to rise to the top.

And there is more. Servius Tullius was the first to arrange a census of the Roman citizens, officially registering them in the citizen body and categorizing them in different positions matching their wealth. He used this census for organizing the Roman army and the voting and elections system. The army was organized in 193 'centuries,' characterized by the sort of equipment the soldiers used. The equipment was linked to the census category. It was supposed that the richer the soldier was, the more massive and valuable equipment he could provide for himself. Eighty centuries of men were classified from the richest, in a full kit of heavy bronze armor; to the fifth class that was equipped with just slings and stones.

According to Livy, the Roman Republic was mostly founded on the efforts and achievements of Servius Tullius. But Livy had something more interesting to tell about, and this was the most controversial part of the story. Servius Tullius had two daughters, and both were called Tullia -Tullia the Elder (Major) and Tullia the Younger (Minor). He wanted them to marry the sons of Tarquin, the Elder, and so they did. But Tullia the Younger and Lucius Tarquinius (married to Tullia, the Elder) arranged the murders of their siblings, then married and plotted the assassination of Servius Tullius. Coldblooded Tullia encouraged her husband to convince senators secretly, and he went to the senate-house followed by a group of armed men. Lucius Tarquinius gathered the senators and gave a speech condemning Servius, pointing out that ultimately he was a slave born of a slave. He said Servius had failed to be selected by the Senate and throughout an interregnum, which was the tradition for the election of kings of Rome, and was, instead, gifted the throne by a woman. Moreover, Tarquin criticized Tullius for supporting the lower classes over the wealthy. Tullius indeed took large parts of the land of the upper classes and distributed it to the poor. Tarquin was not happy about instituting the census either, as it exposed the affluent upper classes to lower classes' envy.

The king came to the senate-house determined to defend his position, but he had no opportunity to speak. Tarquinius threw him down the steps and ordered his men to murder Servius in the street. As if it was not enough, Tullia came with her chariot and drove over her father's body. Tarquinius even refused to allow Tullius's burial, which earned him the nickname "Arrogant" or "Proud" (Superbus).

Tullia Minor Drives over the Corpse of her Father[xiii]

The Arrogant King and the Death of Roman Monarchy

The last Roman king was the son of Tarquinius Priscus, Lucius Tarquinius Superbus, known as 'Tarquin the Proud'- a distrustful tyrant who mercilessly liquidated his opponents. He was married to Servius' daughter, but he overthrew him and grabbed all power. He ruled by fear, ignoring the Senate, which had already been established and had the function of advising the king.

Tarquin the Proud (or Tarquin the Arrogant) selfishly exploited the Roman people and forced them to work on his building projects. The behavior of this king and his family eventually led to public revolt. The breaking point was another rape – one of king's sons, Sextus Tarquinius, raped the virtuous Lucretia. The innocent victim killed herself with a knife, and the revolution had begun, which brought the end of monarchy and the establishment of the 'free Republic of Rome' in late sixth century BC.

The man who drew forth the knife that stabbed Lucretia's heart was Lucius Junius Brutus, the ancestor of a more famous Brutus – the conspirator against Julius Caesar. Brutus gathered the Roman people and banished Tarquin and his family. In 510 BC, the Roman monarchy was over. Two elected consuls replaced the king at the top of society, and the Roman Republic was founded. The first two consuls were Collatinus, the widower of the unfortunate Lucretia (and formerly a close friend to Tarquin's sons), and Brutus.

The Romans vs. the Kings

Ancient Romans had a somewhat problematic relationship with their history, especially with their kings. Tarquinius Superbus was widely loathed and, after his spectacular fall, kings became an object of hatred. There was nothing more dangerous politically than to be accused of wanting to be called a king. Even the emperors were highly cautious and would never tolerate being called a king. But Roman writers saw this issue slightly differently. They recognized the regal period as the source of their major religious and political institutions. Romulus founded the city, and other kings developed it. Even though they were later despised, kings were recognized as the creators of Rome. This was sometimes exaggerated. Rome's ancient historians tended to depict the regal period as more modern and its achievements as more grandiose than they were or even could be.

Chapter 3 – Early Republic

The Dawn of Liberty

Contemporaries and many ancient historians celebrated the end of the monarchy as the birth of freedom as well as of the free Roman Republic. The city of Rome had a fresh start – as a 'public thing' (*res publica*). A new form of government was established. Brutus and Collatinus (the latter was unfortunately exiled shortly after because of his family links; he was, in fact, another Tarquin, and his full name was Lucius Tarquinius Collatinus) became the first consuls of Rome. Consuls were the central public officials of the Republic, in charge of many aspects that used to be the duties of the king. They managed the city politics and were military generals. In a way, their role was very similar to the one of a king and their power was sometimes seen as a 'monarchical' quality in the Roman political system. Their emblems and symbols of the office looked very much like those of their kingly predecessors. But there was a considerable difference between the two political regimes. Consuls were chosen entirely by the vote of the people of Rome, and they could hold the function for only a single year at a time. One of their responsibilities was to preside over the election of their successors. Finally, the power of consuls was both limited and temporary; it was always shared between two consuls and lasted up to a year.

It remains unclear though how and when exactly did the *res publica* begin. Livy and other ancient historians presented a clear narrative of what was most likely to be chaos. Were Brutus and Collatinus the first consuls or were they just said to be so by much later Romans? Most probably, the latter was the case. Ancient writers loved to imagine their traditional institutions went back much further than they did.[xiv] Contrary to the much-celebrated tradition, the new order and the entirely different form of government could not be established instantly. It was a slow, gradual and messy process that lasted for centuries. Rome's representative institutions took shape at some point between 500 BC (the end of the Tarquins) and 300 BC (the time of Scipio 'Long-Beard'). During this period, the Romans slowly defined the underlying principles of Republican politics and civil liberties. They formulated 'what it was to be Roman' and their 'way of doing things' that characterized their subsequent imperial expansion. The most important element that distinguished Rome from every other classical city-state was their idea of citizenship, civil rights, and responsibilities, which still survives in our times. Somewhere during these two centuries, Rome finally began to look 'Roman.'[xv]

The Clash that Defined Rome: The Conflict of Orders and the Twelve Tables

So, what happened during those two hundred years? The fifth and fourth centuries BC were full of internal and external conflicts and tensions. The internal politics of the early Roman Republic are characterized by a dispute between the patricians and the plebeians. The modern term for this clash is the 'Conflict of the Orders.' The old story goes as it follows. After the expulsion of Tarquinius Superbus, the power fell into the hands of a group of aristocratic families collectively known as the patricians.[xvi] Only members of these families could hold religious and political office. They were the ones who elected (among themselves) two annual magistrates called 'consuls' and sometimes during crisis selected a dictator to take sole charge of military matters. Then, at some point between

494 and 287, patrician power and supremacy were challenged by plebeian protest.[xvii]

The antagonism between the patricians and the plebeians was not simply the antipathy between the rich and the poor. The plebeians were not just Rome's poor. All Roman citizens who were not the members of any of the very few patrician families (such as Claudii, Julii, and Cornelii) were categorized as plebeians. Some of them were wealthy, and they were not very happy to accept that they didn't participate in governmental structures. They required an equal share of political power. Even though they could not use the existing political system (which was entirely controlled by the patricians), they had the support of most of the Roman people.

The poorer Romans struggled to maintain their farms during their military service. Some of them turned to patricians for help and fell into debt. That way, they became vulnerable and open to abuse by their creditors. Poor people were becoming slaves to patricians, and their position became unsustainable. In 494 BC the plebeians revolted against the patrician treatment of those among them who fell into debt.[xviii] So they decided to go on strike. When the consuls ordered out the army in 494 BC, the plebeians refused to come. Instead, they met outside Rome and refused to join the army until the patricians granted them some form of representation. This event is known as the First Secession of the Plebs. The patricians had no choice but to make concessions. They gave the plebeians the right to form the Concilium Plebis and to choose their officials – the tribunes – to protect their rights. This was a first major victory of the plebs, but their position was still far from perfect. The patricians still controlled the law (there was no written legal code at the time; the patricians preserved customary unwritten law and judged by it) and the plebeians were still exposed to exploitation. The first written law called the Twelve Tables was composed in 450 BC, because of the revolt against arbitrary patrician justice. The plebeians could know the law for the first time in Roman history, and their position increasingly improved.

The Twelve Tables had some awkward details. Mixing the classes was, for example, strictly forbidden. Intermarriage between patricians and plebeians was not allowed. Some more important laws were passed in subsequent years. It was no longer possible to enslave a Roman citizen for debt. All citizens were granted the right of *provocatio ad populum*, which meant they could appeal to the people against decisions made by a magistrate. In 449 BC (and again in 287 BC) a law declared the entire population (both the patricians and the plebeians) was to be subject to plebiscites. In 445, the law that forbade intermarriage between the classes was revoked. In the next couple of decades, consuls were frequently replaced by several military tribunes with consular power. In years between 391 and 367, there were six consular tribunes,[xix] and plebeians were eligible for election to this function just like patricians.[xx] 367 BC brought a series of changes and new laws. In the years that followed, plebeians were frequently elected as consuls, dictators[xxi], censors, pontiffs, praetors, and augurs. Starting from 342 BC, plebeians had access to nearly all significant political and religious offices. There was still the distinction between the classes by birth, but a new Roman aristocracy emerged. The new ruling class consisted of both patrician and plebeian wealthy families.

As for the poorer plebeians, they were yet to wait for the better times. Their interests were different from those of their leaders. These leaders were men of substantial property, and they aspired to be politically powerful. Wealthy plebeians wanted to contribute to the Roman institutions from which birth excluded them, and they made it. Patrician exclusivity was diminished. Step by step, new reforms, and legislation allowed plebeians to marry patricians and vice versa. The plebeian elite had equal rights as patricians by 300 BC. But the Rome's poor still lived in inadequate conditions, which led to another secession of the plebs – the third and final one – in 287 BC.

A republic took shape when laws had been recorded, and the patricians were enforced to acknowledge plebeian rights, institutions, and organizations. A delicate balance of power had been created, and it worked most of the time. But it did now work flawlessly. Tribunes – the officials of the plebs – had an important power at their discretion: the veto. They could use this power to impede anything against the interests of the plebeians. However, those of plebeians who were wealthy and powerful enough to get themselves elected as tribunes had the interests that were similar to the ones of patricians, rather than the ones of underprivileged plebeians. The reforms we've just mentioned were just a step towards the maturity of the republic, which fully developed during the next two centuries.

Everyday Lives of Ordinary Romans in the Republic

The highest and most sacred duty of all free Roman men, whether patricians or plebeians, was the one toward their country. They were obliged to enter military service whenever needed; accordingly, going to war and coming back home in victory was the highest honor that brought social prestige and glory. Saving the state from peril and increasing its glory and wealth was deeply ingrained in Roman ethos. Military achievements were also the most convenient way for the plebeians to climb up the social ladder and become novi homines, or new men – that is, to become senators or even consuls, endowing their families with newly forged nobility. That is the reason why Roman social hierarchy was not so stiff and rigid as it was in most other ancient societies. That is probably one of the reasons for Rome's political and military supremacy in its brightest days. When the Empire started to collapse, many Romans interpreted it because of utter moral degradation within the nobility and their putting personal interest and wealth before their office and service to the state.

Citizenship was not taken for granted in the Roman Republic. On the contrary, it was a public display of one's merit. Only property-owning males could be citizens and have the right to vote. However, non-citizens performed a significant role in Rome's economy. Slaves brought from Roman military conquests were a large machinery that performed all menial duties, farmed lands, maintained wealthy homes, educated patrician children, labored in mines. Hundreds of thousands of slaves were brought from foreign campaigns. According to some historians, it was precisely the reliance on slaves that hindered Rome's technological improvement and contributed to its downfall. However, Romans took advantage of the diversity within their slave caste; educated war prisoners were held as educators, teachers, and domestic servants, whereas those who were regarded as barbarians were committed to heavy physical labor on farms and in mines. Through exceptional conduct or some great achievement, slaves could earn the right to freedom, hard as it was to do; however, even then this freedom would not be complete. They would still be obliged to obey their former masters and be loyal to them.

The second sacred locus was family. It incorporated the social status of its members as well as the general Roman ethos which dictated rigid hierarchy. A man's social status and affiliation to a specific family were reflected in his name, fusing his public figure and private identity. On the other hand, women had only one name that was simply derived from their father's second name – for example, the daughter of Publius Cornelius Scipio was simply called Cornelia. The pater familias was the decision maker and absolute master of his household, family, and all other family members, their lives, and liberty. He had legal power and authority over all the family's affairs. He could even kill his wife or children or sell them into slavery without any legal consequences. His ancestors, even dead, were regarded as a significant and active factor in his present; their death masks often hanged from the walls in his home, reminding him of his heritage and duties. The atrium was a unique mix of public and private, as a place where meetings were held, and business was conducted.

Accordingly, upper-class marriage was not a private bond between two people who loved each other. Considering the importance of family, marriage was to enforce the family and contribute to its wellbeing. So, it was regarded as an economic and political matter that was arranged by the elders of the two involved families. Marriages were often arranged between children for the future when they should come of age. Age discrepancy was not a problem; Julius Caesar married his teenage daughter to Pompeus who was a few years his senior to strengthen the two families' political bonds. Grooms would bring their brides to their homes to extend the family line within the nucleus of their heritage – and that was their ancestral home.

Women in Rome

There isn't much of written evidence about women, as they were mainly confined to their homes and domestic roles of wives, daughters and household managers. Even those who were free-born, they were always under the complete authority of their fathers and husbands. Exceptions include the Vestals, virgin priestesses in the temples of Vesta, the goddess of the hearth. Their primary role was to maintain the sacred flame, and so they were widely respected, but also harshly punished if they neglected their duty in any way. Their office was not for a lifetime by definition; they could marry and bear children later in life if they wished. As for regular upper-class women, they usually didn't have property – or if they had, it was entirely at their husbands' disposal. They could inherit money from their fathers, and they were usually given dowry when they married. The dowry was the only female possession that was entirely in her hands to do with it as she pleased. If the husband should have to borrow that money, he was obliged to pay it back to her as soon as the circumstances allowed him.

Patrician women could be highly educated, but most of them never got the chance to demonstrate their worth, not having had a chance to participate in the public life. Even if a woman held public respect and prominence, it was only due to her father's or husband's social standing. For example, the aforementioned Cornelia was widely respected as the daughter of Scipio, the wife of Tiberius Gracchus and subsequently the mother of the Gracchi brothers. As such, she was regarded as a paradigm of woman's virtue in ancient Rome – as a paragon of loyalty, modesty, nobility, and fertility, as a mother of twelve and thus a perfect example of a matron.

Public Life

Public life was extraordinarily vivid and developed in Ancient Rome. It was largely financed by the Senate and wealthy patricians who considered it their duty to build public baths, theaters, amphitheaters for gladiatorial games, to sponsor and organize chariot races and other means of entertainment for the city masses. Public baths were not only built in cities but even in villages and other small communities. Gladiatorial games were very symptomatic of Rome's evolution over the centuries; at first, they were part of funeral ceremonies and included only a few fighters to honor the deceased man. With time, they evolved into large, expensive and extravagant public spectacles financed by emperors and magistrates to earn public favor and popularity. They often lasted even for months, with thousands of gladiators butchering each other and the wild animals in front of enthusiastic spectators.

Religion and rituals permeated all spheres of public and private life. In its major part, it was adopted from the Greeks who had inhabited Italian peninsula in the early days of Rome. Thus, the major god was Jupiter, a Roman version of Zeus and Juno, his wife, derived from Greek Hera. The war god Mars was the equivalent of Greek Ares and Venus for the Greek goddess of love and beauty Aphrodite. But there were also many deities adopted from other cultures, such as Sabine Quirinus, who was regarded as the god of the Roman state. All major political and military decisions were followed by sacrifices to the gods, seeking their approval, protection, and blessing; March, as the first month of the year, was brimming with festivals to celebrate the opening of the new season of war campaigns. Romans' everyday life was also infused with the influence of minor spirits who were believed to be the guardians of their homes – such as Lares and Penates. Every household had a small sanctuary devoted to those spirits. Rituals were considered the most important way to summon the gods and connect with them. To foresee the future, Roman priests (*augures* and *haruspices*) watched the skies observing the weather conditions, the birds' flight and examined the entrails of sacrificed animals, much like the Etruscans used to do. To maintain the *pax deorum* (the peace of the gods) and bring the gods to their side, they held annual festivals, in which all of the citizens participated.

Chapter 4 – Military Achievements of Early Republic: Taking Italy

Rome was in an almost constant state of war – just as were other Italian cities and states. That is why the secessions of plebs had such profound results: Rome needed these men to perform their military service.

The Roman army fought first against the neighboring tribes, Etruscans, Samnites, and others within Italy. In the ages that were yet to come, the Romans dominated the Mediterranean and places as distant as Britannia and Asia Minor. But at the beginning, Rome simply needed to secure its borders and maintain internal order during civil wars.

The Romans did not start off with a master-plan on how to conquer the world. The first wars in the early Roman Republic were mostly of defense. Rome protected itself from surrounding cities and peoples, but it also established its territory in the region.[xxii] At the very beginning of the Republic, Etruscan armies attacked Rome twice. The overthrown king Tarquin the Proud was Etruscan, and he initiated these attacks to reclaim his throne, or to avenge the people of Rome who expelled him. The Romans fought bravely and won. The Romans' defense impressed and inspired other Latin cities and in (approx.) 506 BC they created the Latin League, determined to get rid of the Etruscans for good. Thirty cities (excluding Rome) collaborated and fought together. The Etruscans attacked the League as soon as it was formed, but with no success. The joint effort worked; the League cut the Etruscans off from southern Italy at the Battle of Aricia and weakened the Etruscans permanently.

Despite the shared enemy, the League and Rome were not allies, at least not at the beginning. The reason was obvious – the Latins were not quite happy about Rome's growing power. The two sides fought at Lake Regillus in 496 BC, but the battle ended as soon as it began, due to politics. The Latins needed Rome's help against mountain tribes that were coming down and invading their land. They made a deal and, consequently, the Latin cities became a part of the Roman system.

The Gauls

The new threat came from Gaulish Celts around 390 BC. The Gauls entered northern Italy and menaced the Etruscan city of Clusium. The Etruscans needed help from Rome, and it came. Rome chased off the invaders, but soon after that, a Gaulish army returned, reaching the river Allia just 15 kilometers (approx.) north of Rome. The armies met, and the Gauls won, causing serious damage to the Roman army, land, and economy. This was a tough lesson for Rome, but substantial for its maturing. A series of economic and political changes took place, and the influence of the plebs increased further. The Roman citizenship was given to many newcomers, as well as ex-slaves (who had no voting rights, but their children did). At the same time, the importance of military service had been additionally highlighted. The Romans were determined to repair the damage and grow strong again. They learned their lesson well and decided that no one would ever capture Rome again. Massive walls[xxiii] were built to prevent anyone from invading the city. When the Gauls came to invade Rome again in 360 BC, they couldn't penetrate the walls and, after a while just turned back home. The construction of the walls was not the only Roman means of defense. They restructured the army entirely to make it more capable of resisting a high-speed barbarian attack. Small, flexible units replaced cumbersome infantry.

Troops were armed with javelins and swords. From a merely defensive force, the Roman army grew to become a threatening force. So, when the Etruscans, encouraged by the Gauls' invasion of 360 BC, tried to invade Rome again, the Romans – now the regional leaders – reorganized the Latin League and defeated Etruscans once for all.

The Samnites

The Romans and the Latins were situated in the plains west of the Apennine Mountains, which were the home to several tribes collectively known as the Samnites. They entered each other's territories, and the clash was inevitable. Fearing from another Gaulish invasion, the two sides signed a treaty in 354 BC, but they were not allies for long. When the Samnites began pestering the Campanian city of Capua, Capuans asked Rome for help. The Romans were enthusiastic about the chance to gain the control over the whole region of Campania, so they turned sides and scared away the Samnites from Capua and the surrounding area. The so-called First Samnite War lasted from 343 to 341 BC and ended without a winner. Neither the Romans nor the Samnites could persist and keep fighting. Both sides needed to cope with their problems. The Romans had to deal with a mutiny within the army because the soldiers were not willing to be away from home for such a long time. The Samnites, on the other hand, were exposed to attacks from Tarentum, a Greek colony in southern Italy. The treaty between the Romans and the Samnites was renewed, but another threat was on the way. The Latins saw a chance in the Roman's army mutiny, made an alliance with the Campanians and the Volsci, and demanded the reinstatement of equality between themselves and Rome. But the Romans were not as vulnerable as they seemed. They used their agreement with the Samnites to overwhelm both the Latins and Campanians. After that, the Romans made a deal with the Campanians and, finally, pulled the Latin League apart. The technique called divide and rule – turning one tribe against another – was the Romans' specialty. Each city that used to be a part of the

Latin League was forced to face Rome individually and accept a profound change in their status. In 338 BC, they all became the municipiae (municipalities) or colonies of Rome. These cities preserved their identities and partial local autonomy, but their inhabitants became a part of the Roman legislative system.

The mighty Romans made a deal with the Greek city of Tarentum, which was, an enemy to the Samnites. The Samnites then made peace with Tarentum, attacked the Greek port of Neapolis and indirectly threatened the Capuans who, in turn, asked Rome for help. The Romans came, and the Second Samnite War began in 326 BC. The Samnite garrison had to give up their plan to invade the plains of the western coast, and they returned to Samnium. Nothing significant happened during the next couple of years, but the tension persisted. The Romans felt incapable of fighting in the Samnites' mountain terrain. The Samnites, on the other hand, could not do anything on the plains, weighed down by Roman garrisons. In 321 BC the Romans, eager to fight, directed their garrisons from Capua to attack the Samnites on their land. The Roman army was on the way to Samnium, but the Samnites trapped them and forced them into surrender. The Samnites believed they'd won. However, the Romans quickly regrouped. This was one of the greatest Roman advantages; after each defeat, their army grew larger and strategies enhanced. In 316 BC the Samnites won another battle, but in 314 BC returned the control over the territory around the Mountains. In 304 BC peace was made, but in 298 BC the Third Samnite War began, and it lasted for nearly a decade. The Samnites had the support of the Etruscans and the Gauls. It had been hard to fight such a serious enemy, and the Romans lost battle after battle, but eventually, they managed to kill the Samnite leader Egnatius Gellus. The likely disaster turned out to be the Roman triumph. They made allies first with the Samnite helpers, and at the end with the Samnites – under the Romans' conditions, of course. To be a Roman ally meant to be obliged to contribute to Rome's army.

The Greeks

The Romans gradually gained control of most of Italy. The last to deal with was southern Italy or Magna Graecia ('Great Greece') controlled by the Greek colonies, including Tarentum. The Tarentines were wealthy. Their thriving economy enabled them to handle a huge army. They also had a large navy and could even afford mercenaries to help them when needed. In 334 BC, the rulers of Tarentum hired Alexander of Epirus[xxiv] to help them to resist invasions by the Samnites and Lucanians. Alexander turned out to be more interested in appropriating his own empire, and the Tarentines were not particularly moved when the Lucanians killed him.

The Romans were ambitious, and the Tarentines were worried. Rome's power and influence were enormous. Whenever some place felt under threat, they asked the Romans for help. So, when the Romans sent their ships to a nearby Greek city of Thurii, the Tarentines attacked and overwhelmed them. They were feeling self-assured because they had employed the number one Greek soldier of his day, King Pyrrhus of Epirus, and his army of 25,000 men and 20 war elephants, which were borrowed by the Egyptian ruler Ptolemy II. Pyrrhus won in 280 BC at Heraclea, and again in 279 BC, at Asculum, but it was a costly victory with large loses. From Pyrrhus's perspective, it wasn't worth it. So, he went to fight the Carthaginians instead. Meanwhile, the Romans attacked the Samnites and the Lucanians, who in 276 BC asked Pyrrhus to return and help them. He came, but the Romans defeated him at Beneventum. Aside from the expression 'Pyrrhus's victory,' meaning a victory that just wasn't worth it, Pyrrhus is remembered by his extraordinary death. After all those battles and wars, he participated in, he died by accident, when a pot flanged out of a window fell on his head.

Pyrrhus was history, and the world of possibilities was open for the Romans. In 272 BC they seized Tarentum, and finally gained control of the entire Italian peninsula. All Greek cities had no choice but to enter the Roman system and become *socii* (allies). Just like the Latin cities had to provide troops, the Greek cities provided ships. The peninsula now consisted of Roman colonies.

The Roman supremacy did not go unnoticed by the other powerful armies on the Mediterranean, and both the Carthaginians and the Egyptians were making deals of friendship with the Roman Republic.

Chapter 5 – Middle Republic: The Punic Wars and Mediterranean Dominance

By 275 BC the Roman Republic was firmly established and its political and social structures fully defined. The joint leadership of the Senate granted stability and directed the ambitions of the elite. The populace had a voice through assemblies and elections. In return, the ordinary Romans willingly contributed to military campaigns. The large network of Roman allies, ranging from the nearby Latin cities and tribes to the ones on the south, previously known as Magna Graecia, enlarged the Rome's power and gave it control over all of Italy. However, the Republic was still just a regional player, not a Mediterranean one. But this changed during the 3rd century BC. The expansion of Roman prospects outside Italy got Rome into direct conflict with a terrifying enemy – Carthage in North Africa. Rome fought against Carthage in the Punic War between 264 and 146 BC. The Roman Republic was almost destroyed in dramatic twists and turns, but it won in the end, becoming a genuine Mediterranean power.

The Phoenicians (*Punici*) and Carthage

Ancient Carthage has been thoroughly ruined, and we know nothing about their point of view regarding the Punic wars. We interpret their motives and actions through the historical texts written by Livy and

Polybius.[xxv] After all, history has always been written by the victors, especially in the ancient times when great civilizations were ruined leaving no written accounts of their own. Hence for us, the Phoenicians were simply the foes of Rome. But thanks to Roman historians, however biased they might be, we know more about this remarkable ancient society.

Carthage was indeed mighty. The city was founded in c. 800 BC by Phoenicians, who came from the eastern city of Tyre (present-day Lebanon) and were specialized in maritime trading. Carthage was located on a first-class natural harbor on the cape that today belongs to the city of Tunis. Carthage controlled entire trade in the western Mediterranean, and according to Polybius, was 'the richest city in the world.' Its moneymaking empire spread across North Africa, into Spain, and (then Greek, now Italian) islands of Sardinia and Sicily.

While Rome relied primarily on agriculture, the people of Carthage were devoted to trade and industry. The political and military structures of the two sides were equally different. Rome was, as we have elaborated, a fully developed republic, and Carthage was an oligarchy, with its wealthiest families at the top. Its army consisted of mercenaries – Numidia's elite cavalry and even North African elephants – directed by Carthaginian officers. Carthage particularly relied on its remarkable navy, roughly 200 *quinquiremes*, magnificent, 45 meters long galleys, each carrying 120 battle marines. With such impressive and efficient navy and well-trained men, Carthage controlled the western Mediterranean for years. And then the Romans emerged.

The First Punic War

As the Roman Republic grew stronger, a rivalry with Carthage was inevitable. The two forces were in good terms with each other at the beginning; they even signed a treaty during the Pyrrhic war. This alliance was a useful means against Pyrrhus's aggression, but after he was defeated the things changed drastically. Rome now controlled all of Italy including its southmost area and, naturally, its activities spread on Sicily, which was under the Carthaginian domain. For centuries Carthage fought against the Syracusan and other Greeks to achieve dominance. But now a band of Italian mercenaries called *the sons of Mars* (*Mamertines*) conquered the Sicilian city of Messina and attacked both Carthaginian and Syracusan territory. The attacks started in 288 BC, and in 265 BC opposing factions within Messina asked Rome and Carthage for help. Carthage sent a fleet, but a Roman army came into Sicily and forced the Carthaginian commander to surrender the town. Syracuse joined Rome against Carthage, and thus the First Punic War began in 264 BC.

Rome's ambitions

It is easy to understand why the Carthaginians sent a fleet to help Messina; they had a long history of involvement in the region. But why did the Romans come? There are several possible answers. Rome might have been frightened by the prospects of the Carthaginians' dominance in Sicily. Or they were driven by *fides* (good faith) and felt they needed to support their allies in times of danger. According to ancient sources – including the contemporary Romans themselves – they fought only in defense of either their city or their friends. But was that all? There was also the fact the Romans just loved war. Its society appreciated the economic rewards of conquest, and the elite fought for military glory. The consuls personally led the armies and the Senate, which made all the decisions and pushed Rome towards warfare.

Fighting at sea

After the opening clash over Messina, both sides were idle for a while. Carthage was focused on defending the coastal towns, and the Romans couldn't approach them from the land. Meanwhile, the Carthaginian navy started attacking the Italian coast. The Romans had a few ships, but not a proper navy, and now was the perfect time to start constructing one. So, they did it. Within 60 days, the Romans built 120 quinquiremes. The Romans themselves did not have much experience at sea, but the allies from southern Italy did, so they became the crew of new Roman ships. In 260 BC at Mylae, the Rome's fleet achieved a great victory. They captured 50 Carthage ships and demolished them; the bronze was used to decorate a column in the Roman Forum in honor of Gaius Duilius.

Rome had suddenly become a serious naval force, and then everything changed. The Romans recognized an opportunity, and in 256–255 BC sent an army to Africa to attack Carthage, but without success. Carthaginian mercenaries led by the Spartan Xanthippus crushed the Roman army, and the support from the sea got caught in a severe storm, 280 ships with over 100,000 men were lost. More fleets fell victims to storms in the following years; the Carthaginians beat others. The war was long and exhaustive, both sides suffered substantial losses, and neither was winning. The consequences were felt in Rome. Roughly 20 percent of Italian men had passed away, either in battles or storms. Nevertheless, Rome was unwilling to discuss peace. Instead, the legislative institutions raised the taxes and ordered the aristocrats to give loans with no exceptions. Every three senators had to provide a warship. As a result, a brand-new fleet was built. In 241 BC, close to the Aegates Islands (which belonged to western Sicily), this fleet won a final naval victory. The war was over, and the Carthaginians were forced to leave Sicily and pay reparation of 3,200 silver talents (roughly one hundred tons of silver). Carthage was economically devastated, and its mercenaries revolted. Meanwhile, the Romans took Sardinia, and then requested 1,200 talents from Carthage, or else they would restart the war.

The end of the First Punic War additionally confirmed Rome's power. The Roman Republic proved itself to be resilient in hard times, able to deal with both military and economic pressure. Moreover, the net of Roman allies functioned well. The loyalty had been confirmed, and the links strengthened. As for Sicily, it became the first tax-paying province of Rome. This was not the only difference in status between Sicily and Roman ally cities in Italy. A Roman preator must govern this area, and a Roman quaestor got the job to oversee taxation. A small garrison stayed there as well, just in case. Other than that, the social and political structures were preserved. The Romans developed a highly flexible system in which political structures of a province remained virtually intact, while Rome ruled through the local elites. This became the standard for all provincial administration under the Roman Republic. Sicily was first, next was Sardinia, and many other places and cities were yet to become Roman provinces.

The Second Punic War: Hannibal and Scipio

After Carthage lost Sicily and Sardinia, its leaders focused on expanding its territory in Spain. The Carthaginians exploited the precious Spanish silver mines to pay the tax that Rome demanded. Spain was under the rule of the Carthaginian general Hamilcar Barca (*Thunderer*) who passionately hated the Romans and sought revenge, as well as restoring Carthaginian dignity. He raised a son teaching him to hate the Romans too. At the age of nine, the young Hannibal swore that he would forever be the foe of Rome. Hannibal was the greatest single enemy that the Republic ever encountered.[xxvi] According to Livy, he was one of the best generals of ancient times; a leader that inspired confidence in his men; both mentally and physically strong; brave and resilient; "unequalled as a fighting man, always the first to attack, the last to leave the field."[xxvii] Livy clearly admired him, but he also pointed out that Hannibal's dark side was just as impressive as his virtues, and highlighted his "inhuman cruelty, [...] perfidy, a total disregard of truth, honor, and religion."[xxviii]

Hannibal led the Carthaginian army into the Second Punic War. It wasn't just a hate campaign driven by his wish for revenge. Rome was alarmed by Carthage's expansion into Spain. The 226 BC treaty fixed the River Ebro as the border between the spheres of interest, but then Rome formed an agreement of friendship with the town of Saguntum, which belonged to the Carthaginian sphere. The war had been provoked by Hannibal's attack upon Saguntum in 219 BC.

Rome required Hannibal to surrender, but the request was declined, so the Second Punic War began in 218 BC.

Rome and Carthage had different ideas about where the fighting was going to start. The Romans were preparing to attack Carthaginian land in both Spain and North Africa, but Hannibal had already started marching for the Alps. His idea was to invade Italy, Rome's source of men and resources. His way was risky; he needed to cross the Alpine mountains, during which more than half his men and a number of elephants died. But Hannibal was determined. He managed to enter Italy with his finest warriors, and then the Gauls from Cisalpine (the town that had just been added to the Roman system and wasn't entirely happy about it) joined him.

Hannibal's triumphs; the battle at Cannae

Hannibal inflicted huge losses on the Romans in Italy. First, in November 218 BC, his Numidian cavalry won a battle at the River Ticinus because the Roman army led by the consul Sempronius Longus was late and didn't have a chance to fight. Once the Romans finally arrived, in December, they attacked the Carthaginians at the River Trebia and were devastated. 20,000 Romans died, Hannibal proclaimed victory and the 'liberation' of Rome's allies and released all his Italian prisoners (those from the Roman "ally" cities) without ransom. The Romans didn't care about his propaganda and attacked him again in the spring. Gaius Flaminius, one of that year's (217 BC) elected consuls, led the army, which pursued the Carthaginians through Etruria, and then fell into a trap at the Lake Trasimene. Hannibal's cavalry came from the back and cut the Romans off. 15,000 men, including Flaminius, were either killed in conflict or drowned. This situation required special measures. Rome appointed a dictator, Quintus Fabius Maximus. His nickname Cunctator means 'Delayer.', His strategy included avoiding open battle and finding a way to make Hannibal exhausted. This strategy was profoundly different from the Roman style of fighting, and Fabius had no support within his lines, so he was unable to prevent Hannibal entering southern Italy. In 216, the newly elected consuls, Lucius Aemilius Paullus and Gaius Terentius Varro led the Roman forces to encounter Hannibal at Cannae. This battle was the greatest Republican defeat for over a century.[xxix] Even though there were two times more Romans than Carthaginians, Hannibal managed to encircle, trap and slaughter them. Hannibal then continued advancing and was only six miles from Rome.

The Battle of Cannae was Hannibal's greatest success that assured his reputation as a military genius. Now his propaganda began to have an effect, and he won over many of Rome's allies, mostly the Greek colonies in southern Italy and Syracuse in Sicily. However, he still had no sufficient power to attack the city of Rome itself. Also, he failed to win over all of Rome's allies; most Italian people and cities remained loyal to Rome.

The changes in Roman tactics

Meanwhile, in Rome, it became clear the Republican system of annually elected magistrates didn't work at war. Fabius Maximus Cunctator was restored to power together with the aggressive Marcus Claudius Marcellus. They became known as the 'Shield and Sword of Rome.' Rome was recovering. Up to that point, the Carthaginians had killed over 70,000 Romans in a short period of just three years. But by 212 BC, a new army of 200,000 Roman soldiers in Italy, Sicily, and Spain was ready to confront Hannibal. Approximately 50,000 men were positioned only to stalk Hannibal's army, which was hugely outnumbered. The Romans had the mission to restrict the Carthaginians' progressing and suppress those who joined their side. The Romans were determined to win this war.

Hannibal's movements in Italy were restricted, and Rome's army won some great victories attention. Marcellus regained Roman control over Syracuse in 211 BC, and soon after that, over entire Sicily, but got killed in 208 in Italy by another of Hannibal's surprise attacks. It felt like victory for the Carthaginians, so they made a major attempt to strengthen Hannibal's army. A relief force led by

Hannibal's brother Hasdrubal came close but was crashed at the River Metaurus in 207 BC. Hasdrubal was murdered and his head thrown into Hannibal's camp. Meanwhile, decisive events were taking place on another front – in Spain.

Rome's new blood: Scipio Africanus

While Hannibal was kept busy in Italy, two Roman generals, the brothers Publius and Gnaeus Cornelius Scipio led an army that opened a series of attacks upon Carthage's possessions in Spain. When 211 BC the Carthaginians killed them in battle, Publius's son also named Publius Cornelius Scipio took over as head of the army. Something like that never happened before in the history of Rome. The young Scipio was only 24 years old. Not only had he never held a public office; he was still ineligible to apply for a position of authority. On the other hand, he was brave, an excellent soldier, and unusually popular within the Roman society.

Scipio instantly restructured the forces in Spain. He introduced new weapons like the Spanish short sword called the gladius and the pilum. Moreover, he reorganized the Roman legion and made its formation more flexible. This new army was highly efficient at the rough terrain of Spain and would shortly prove equally successful against inflexible Greek phalanx. Scipio and his men crossed 250 miles in only five days and attacked the unsuspecting Carthaginians at Nova Carthago (modern Cartagena). Scipio realized the town's fortifications were weak on the coastal side, so he crossed the water at low tide and conquered Nova Carthago in 209 BC. Rome, therefore, took the control over the abundant silver mines close to the city. By 205 BC, Carthaginian forces had been expelled from Spain.

Scipio returned home in 205 BC, welcomed as the true hero of Rome. Thanks to immense popularity and public support, despite the objections of older senators led by Fabius Maximus, he became a consul and got chosen to lead the previously planned Roman invasion of North Africa. Hannibal had to return to his city after 30 years, to defend it from the Romans. The Romans, on the other side, managed to win the support of the Numidians, despite their historic alliance with Carthage. Scipio's army won the victory in the final battle of Zama in 202 BC. The Romans did not destroy the city of Carthage, but it was severely damaged, and its power was diminished. This was the greatest Roman victory so far. In commemoration of this remarkable triumph, Publius Cornelius Scipio took the name Africanus.

The aftermath of the Second Punic War

The Second Punic War confirmed once again the strength of the Roman Republic and the extraordinary loyalty of its Italian allies. Hannibal was indeed an incomparable military genius, but even he could not compete with the resilience of the Romans. Rome could absorb the losses and continue fighting until it won. But that does not mean there were no consequences the people of Rome were forced to endure. Numerous people died, families suffered, and so did Rome's dominant industry – agricultural production. At the same time, the increasing wealth the Roman expansion brought caused internal instability within the Republic in the following century.

Scipio Africanus represented a large change in the Roman establishment. His authority and military glory overshadowed the Senate. He became a consul at the age of 30. He had never met the formal criteria, as he never held a junior governmental position. Moreover, he was given command ahead of the aristocrats from the previous generation, like Fabius Maximus. Scipio's extraordinary achievement made him hard to compete against. And many were yet to try, including Julius Caesar and Emperor Augustus.

The end of Carthage

Rome came into conflict with Carthage one final time in the 2nd century BC. This conflict is sometimes called Third Punic War, but it was just a sad epilogue to their decades of rivalry. Carthage was partially recovering until 195 BC when the Romans requested

Hannibal's extradition. To avoid extradition, Hannibal went into exile. That was not the worst thing that happened to the Carthaginians. All military activities were forbidden for them because those were the terms of Carthage's surrender to Rome. Numidia abused this terms by continually seizing Carthaginian territory. The Carthaginians asked Rome for help several times, but the appeal was rejected every time. After the complete indemnity had been paid to Rome, in 151 BC, Carthage fought Numidia. Shortly after that, a Roman embassy led by Marcus Porcius Cato, the Elder arrived to investigate the issue. Upon returning to Rome, Cato declared that Carthage posed a significant danger to Rome and should be destroyed. His famous words *Carthage must be destroyed* (*Carthago delenda est*) became the conclusion of his every speech in the Senate. As a result, Rome again sent its forces to Carthage in 149 BC. The Carthaginians consented to every request, released 300 hostages and handed over all their weapons. This was still not enough for the Romans. They demanded the Carthaginians leave their homes. They were supposed to build a new city at least 10 miles from the sea. This was too much for the unfortunate people of Carthage, so they started fighting out of desperation and endured, with enormous effort, for three years. The annoyed Romans chose another underage consul – the adopted grandson of Scipio Africanus, Publius Cornelius Scipio Aemilianus – who finally broke and destroyed Carthage, and enslaved all surviving people. The Romans went even further; they cursed the ground that used to be Carthage and sowed it with salt. Finally, entire North Africa became a province of the Roman Republic.

Chapter 6 – The Military vs. Cultural Dominance: The Roman Civilization meets the Greek World

After the spectacular triumph over Carthage, the Roman Republic became the leading power of the western Mediterranean. It ruled over entire Italy, Sicily, Sardinia, Spain, and North Africa. But its influence wasn't limited by the borders of its provinces. The Roman Republic oppressed the neighboring areas through political, economic, and military supremacy. Some minor tribes still resisted the influence of Rome, but after Carthage had fallen, no enemy posed a direct threat to the Republic.

In the ancient Mediterranean, the centers of power used to be in the east. The Greek city-states were not nearly as powerful anymore as they were in their best ages, but the sophistication of any civilization was still measured by comparing to the Greek standard. The Greek language, culture, art, philosophy, and literature confirmed Greek's cultural dominance.

After the conquests of Alexander the Great, the eastern part of the Mediterranean had been split between an always changing number of cities, kingdoms, and leagues. Naturally, during the 2nd century BC, the entire Hellenistic world had to admit the domination of the Romans. Rome's relationship with Greece was twofold. The Romans admired Greek culture, which thoroughly influenced and refined the

Roman world. The fascination with all things Greek existed for centuries. The Etruscans respected and widely copied them. King Tarquin, the Elder on one occasion, sent his sons to the oracle in Delphi for advice. In subsequent centuries, numerous Greek statues were brought to Rome. Even Roman pantheon was altered to match with the Greek gods. Greek literature was translated into Latin, and so on. Greek freedom, on the other hand, was not respected that much and Roman armies crushed those who tried to preserve it.

Greece after Alexander the Great

Alexander the Great died in 323 BC. Before his death, he expressed the last will; he wanted his vast conquests to be ruled by 'the strongest.' That was not one of his best decisions. The empire he built over decades was immediately crushed, thanks to the forces from inside. Alexander's generals, each wanting to be 'the strongest,' fought for control. The empire had become fragmented. Three kingdoms arose in its place: the Antigonid dynasty ruled Macedon, Syria under the Seleucids and Egypt under the Ptolemies. Greece was governed by unions of allied cities. The Aetolian League controlled the area north of the Corinthian Gulf. Peloponnese was under control of the Achaean League. Major Greek city-states, such as Athens and Sparta, as well as few others, remained independent, but their political importance was significantly reduced over the centuries. There were a few more states within the territory of what once was the Alexander's empire, including the island of Rhodes and Pergamum in Asia Minor. These cities had a long history of wars and alliances, many of which Rome was utterly unaware.

The Romans come to Greek territory

Military and politically, no individual Greek state could compare with the Roman Republic. But this time it was not all about brute power. The Greek east had a highly sophisticated culture, and the Romans respected that. The Greeks were acknowledged as the arbiters of civilization. This made things complicated for the

Romans. They did not want merely to invade the Hellenistic world and be seen as barbarians. They wanted to be part of the civilized world. This aspiration influenced Roman behavior and tactic. As a result, the process of conquering the eastern Mediterranean was long and, at moments, very painful.

The armies of the two worlds had met before. The Greek ruler Pyrrhus from Epirus invaded Italy in the early 3rd century BC. Roma managed to resist. Now, after the history of defeating threatening forces from the east – first Pyrrhus's, then Hannibal's army, the Romans directed their attention toward that side of the world. The first conflicts began between the two great Punic Wars when Rome invaded the coastal region of Illyria. Philip V, ruler of the nearby kingdom of Macedon, saw the Romans as a threat (the Illyrian pirates were, after all, his mercenaries) and, after the battle of Cannae, he signed a treaty of cooperation with Hannibal. The so-called First Macedonian War ended quickly – Philip realized Rome was going to win the Second Punic War and signed peace in 205 BC – but two years after they crushed Carthage, the Roman authorities declared war on Macedon. Thus, began the Second Macedonian War.

Rome, Macedon and the freedom of Greece

There were many reasons for Rome to enter the war against Macedon. Philip V, supported by the Seleucid Empire in Syria, wanted to attack Egypt and take power and the wealth away from the underage king Ptolemy V. On the way, Philip's forces harassed everyone else in the Aegean. The Greeks got upset by his actions. Pergamon and Rhodes allied with Philip who, in turn, hammered their joined forces. In 201 BC those Greeks asked Rome for help. But, curiously enough, the people of Rome did not want to fight. The first consul's request for a declaration of war against Macedon was declined in 200 BC by the Comitia Centuriata. Even the Roman elite, which was always eager to fight and attain military glory, was reluctant. But once the word had spread that Phillip was in alliance with the Seleucids, the war was inevitable. The Romans wanted to crush Antiochus the Great of the Seleucids, along with Philip, but they made it look as if their only goal was to protect the Greek cities.

Greeks warmly welcomed the Roman legions. The Aetolian and Achaean Leagues united and stood behind Rome. However, at first, it looked like Philip was winning, but the joint Greek-Roman army led by Titus Quinctius Flamininus managed to defeat the Macedonians at the end. Like Scipio Africanus, Flaminius was only 30 years old. He was a philhellene, an admirer of Greek culture who spoke Greek fluently, and a man capable of winning Greek support and promoting an appropriate image of Rome as a civilized state.

At the Isthmian Games of Corinth in 196 BC, Flamininus gave a speech in Greek and proclaimed the 'Freedom of Greece.' The Greeks were so happy that, as later Roman sources say, their intense shout of joy killed the flying ravens.[xxx] Greeks were so grateful and went so far they honored Flamininus as a god.

At this point, the Romans respected Greek freedom. Rome had withdrawn all its troops by 194 BC. Greek cities did not become new Roman provinces. This was very unusual, but there were two reasons to let Greece alone. First, Rome did not have the resources – either the standing army or the bureaucracy – that would make it possible to administer Greece. And there was also the admiration for Greek culture. Rome initially counted more on diplomacy than direct rule. After all, Greek opinion carried some weight and Rome had to appear 'civilized.' But in 106 BC Rome declared the Greeks were under its protection and hence indirectly challenged Antiochus III of Seleucid Syria, also known as Antiochus the Great. The most prominent of Hellenistic monarchs, Antiochus was a powerful ruler with imperialistic attitude who continuously frightened Pergamum and Rhodes, which were now Rome's allies. In 195 BC Hannibal, who had been banished from Carthage, joined Antiochus, and this additionally concerned the Romans. Meanwhile, the Aetolian League abandoned the alliance with Rome and joined Antiochus who in 191 BC entered Greece.

Rome reacted instantly and crushed Antiochus at Thermopylae, the famous place where the Spartans had fought against the Persians three centuries earlier. The Seleucid army had to retreat into Syria. The new consul Lucius Cornelius Scipio, followed by his brother Scipio Africanus (Lucius won election thanks to Africanus, who promised to serve alongside him) routed the enemy. Rome once again withdrew its troops from Greece, but its power over eastern territories had been confirmed. Antiochus was ordered to surrender Hannibal who meanwhile disappeared, to be found by Flamininus in 183 BC. The old foe of Rome took the poison, so he wouldn't have to surrender to Rome.

Graeco-Roman culture and the tension

Graecia capta ferum victorem cepit et artes intulit agresti Latio.— Horace[xxxi]

Over the next couple of decades, Rome continued with the same policy toward Greek cities – there were no troops, no tributes, and no provinces. The Greek impact on Roman life, on the other hand, increased dramatically. Greek art and literature flooded into Italy. Roman noble households employed Greek teachers. The new hybrid culture was developing, and philhellenes led by Flamininus and Scipio Africanus encouraged it. But there was another stream within Rome, according to which philhellenism posed a threat to Rome's traditional values. Marcus Porcius Cato the Elder and his supporters believed the Greeks were not only inferior to the Romans, but also a source of corruption.

The Republic adopted their hardline politics around 170 BC. From that time onwards, Rome still appreciated Greek culture but expected the Greeks to acknowledge their authority. The Greek cities were expected to act like Rome's Italian allies – they were 'free' to rule themselves, as long as they remained still and acted only when instructed to do so. The Greeks thought otherwise. The Greeks had a long history of rivalries and local conflicts, and this did not stop with the arrival of Rome. The Senate of the Roman Republic now received numerous appeals and had to act as an arbiter in Greek disputes. This was boring and exhaustive for Roma officials, who started supporting causes randomly. The cases that had something to do with Rome were solved in a way that suited Roman interests. Such was the case of Macedon. Perseus of Macedon was driven into the Third Macedonian War and refused to fight against Romans until his kingdom was crushed, even though he was willing to surrender under any conditions.

Rome still wasn't interested in seizing territories or creating provinces in the east, but the Republic required the recognition of its power. After it destroyed Macedon, others felt the force too. The Romans executed 500 leading Aetolians and took 1,000 Achaeans, including the future historian Polybius, as prisoners. 150,000 people from Epirus were enslaved, The power of Pergamum and Rhodes was significantly reduced. Antiochus IV of Syria was requested to abandon his plans of invading Ptolemaic Egypt, and he had no choice but to conform to the will of Rome.

By 167 BC, no one could challenge Roman power. Polybius advised his fellow Greeks to abide by Roman dominance and avoid experiencing 'the fate that awaited those who opposed Rome.'[xxxii] He was correct. All later revolts were brutally crushed. Macedonia finally became a Roman province. Corinth was destroyed in 146 BC, the same year when Carthage faced the same destiny. The days of 'freedom' given to the Greeks in Corinth half a century before were over. Greece, Syria, and Egypt were still not Rome's provinces (but would become so under Augustus), but the Roman Republic effectively ruled over the Greek city-states and the legacy of Alexander the Great.

Chapter 7 – Limitless Power and the Beginning of the End: The Late Republic

By 130s BC, Rome conquered the whole Mediterranean. This was an astonishing achievement. There is no state, ancient or modern, in the world that ever managed to get even close to that. Other ancient societies controlled significantly smaller territories. The Egyptians at the peak of their power weren't much influential beyond the areas of Levant and Asia Minor. The Greeks had many colonies around the Mediterranean, but they lacked centralized control and a well-structured political system that would hold everything together. Romans not only beat them all politically and militarily. It was them, not the Greeks, who spread Greek art, literature, and philosophy all over the world.

At the end of the century, Rome was the most powerful state in the ancient world and beyond. But within another century, the Roman Republic was gone. Those were the years of ambition, corruption, and civil war that threatened to destroy all that had been achieved over the previous centuries. The rich grew richer, the poor became even poorer, and the traditional institutions could not cope with the new challenges.

The origin of crisis

The Roman Republican system was initially established around public services, like consulship. Ideally, because people were elected for public functions year after year, no one individual was supposed to become pre-eminent. It didn't function that way. Individuals could not hold power for a long time, but their families could. The elite that, as we've seen, included the patricians and the most successful plebeian families (*nobiles*), controlled entire political system.

The voting system was seriously flawed. People who lived far away from the city of Rome could not come and vote. As for those who lived inside the city walls, their votes were frequently and routinely bought. The buying of votes was simple. The most powerful individuals called the patrons were surrounded by their *clients*: the ex-slaves that they freed, business associates and other people who needed the protection of a patron. So, the patrons helped and supported their clients, who in turn voted for them without exception. Votes were also bought for cash and through the organization of free public entertainments. As a result, no plebeian could ever enter the Senate.

The angry crowd

Former agricultural workers and smallholders had become soldiers during the times of wars. The problem of workforce in the fields was solved then by bringing slaves. Now the war was over; these men were out of work. The growth of large estates held by the elite and slave labor, small farmers, struggled to keep land of their own. Too many of them were left without anything. Out of desperation, they came to Rome. The growing urban mob was at times hostile and presented a great risk of disorder. The elite that made them poor had to find the way to control them.

There was a similar crisis with the Italian allies. Their people died at battlefields for Rome, and their loyalty was essential for Rome's success, but they received almost nothing in return, and their political influence was heavily limited.

No one wanted to go to war anymore. Both the Romans and the allies tried their best to avoid military service, and this was a large problem, as we will see.

A new class: the equestrians

The very structure of Roman society was changing. Some new wealthy families requested their share of power. The equestrians or equites were initially the knights, Roman citizens rich enough to serve in a cavalry. Meanwhile, they became a separate bloc within the society and a second-grade elite. Even though they did not have the status of old aristocracy, they possessed substantial wealth. From 129, the *ordo equester* was formally separated from the senatorial order, which made it hard (but still possible) for equestrians to become senators. Nevertheless, this social class was involved in lucrative construction projects and the collection of taxes.

The Gracchi

The Gracchi – Tiberius and Gaius Gracchus had the highest aristocratic origin. Their father was the distinguished war commander and was twice elected consul. Their mother Cornelia was the daughter of the Rome's greatest hero, Scipio Africanus. But these noble brothers were determined to reform the same social and political system that had made their families powerful.

Tiberius and Gaius Gracchus made every effort to pass laws that would improve the status of the Roman citizens in Italy and make the distribution of land more just. However, their efforts were against the interest of the Senate and the aristocracy, who used all methods available to weaken them. Eventually, the Gracchi brothers got killed, and the reforms failed. All they managed to do was to make a name for themselves in history as popular Roman martyrs.

Tiberius Sempronius Gracchus, the older of the brothers, was expected to achieve military success and become a consul. But he had other plans. He became a tribune, determined to fight for social justice. In 133 BC, he recommended that abandoned land all around Italy should be given to unemployed small farmers. This measure would solve three acute problems: social tension would be reduced; the urban mob would disperse, and people would be willing to go to army again. But the land he was talking about – the public land taken during conquests – was largely exploited by aristocrats, who employed slaves to work on fields. There was a limitation of how much of the public land could be used by one Roman, and Tiberius wanted to confiscate all land that exceeded that limit and share it among the unemployed people. These properties would be small, but inalienable, and wealthy landowners could not buy them.

The senatorial elite was entirely against this plan. They inherited the public land (paradoxical, but true) for generations and weren't willing to share it with the poor. They used all political power to stop Tiberius, but he brought the law called *Lex Sempronia agrarian*. But this law could not be enforced. Tiberius was alone against many and found himself persistently obstructed.

Meanwhile, King Attalus III of Pergamum died. He had no heirs, and his kingdom now belonged to Rome. Tiberius took this opportunity to subsidize his property redistribution. In a decree in 133 BC, he announced the people – not the government – would govern the new province of Asia. The Roman Republican institutions were challenged, Tiberius was accused of wanting to become a king, which eventually got him killed and thrown into the river Tiber.

In 123 BC, Tiberius' younger brother Gaius won election as tribune. He knew well what he could expect from the senatorial elite, but he, too, pursued the reform that his brother had begun. He also required the redistribution of land to help the small farmers. On the other hand, his ideas were much broader, developed further, and brought prosperity to all levels of Republican society. In the end, he was judged by the Senate, and the first ever final decree of the Senate (senatus consultum ultimum) decided that Gaius' death would in best interest of Rome. His supporters were murdered, and he committed suicide. It was promised that whoever brought Gaius' head would receive its weight in gold. The man who brought the head first took the brain out and filled it with molten lead before requesting the reward. Thus, began the century of chaos, internal tension, and military crisis.

Marius, the first warlord

In 112 BC, Jugurtha, the king of Numidia, and African province of Rome ordered the murder of Roman and Italian traders in the province. This insult caused the beginning of the Jugurthine War. Jugurtha could not compete with Rome military, but he took significant advantage over the corruption and incompetence of Roman generals. According to Jugurtha, Rome was "a city up for sale, and its days are numbered should it find a buyer." The war dragged on until, in 107 BC, Gaius Marius was elected consul and took over command. Marius was known as *a novus homo.* He reached the consulship thanks to his abilities, not his family. He enjoyed a reputation of an experienced soldier, and he beat Jugurtha swiftly. Then a new threat came. Whole tribes of Germans were moving into Roman Territory. Marius fought them successfully, but with enormous casualties. Meanwhile, he reformed the army by letting all volunteers fight. Rome for the first time in history had a permanent army. These new soldiers had neither properties nor obligations at home and could serve for long periods under rigorous discipline. They could not afford to equip themselves since they were poor, so they were all armed alike by the state. Celebrated as the savior of Rome, Marius was elected consul five years in a row. His domination of the consulship was unprecedented status. He became the first in the line of the great warlords who dominated the last decades of the Republic.

The Marian reforms established a professional infantry army, which collided with the old ideal of a Roman citizen militia. The soldiers had no land but were promised a farm at the end of their service. They were loyal to their general, not the Senate. These changes caused the emergence of private armies in the service of men influential enough to keep them. The first to make the advantage of the new possibilities was Lucius Cornelius Sulla, Marius's long-time rival.

The war against allies: The Social War

The status of Rome's Italian allies had not been improved over the years, and they still had no political rights. On the other hand, two-thirds of Marius' soldiers were Italians, not Roman citizens. They demanded Italian Roman citizenship and, when in 91 BC their defender, the tribune Marcus Livius Drusus, was murdered, they initiated the Social War (the Latin term for 'allies' was 'socii'). Their aim was not to demolish Rome but to demand concessions and in 88 BC Rome finally submitted to the demands and war was over.

Sulla's march on Rome

The leading Roman general in this war was Sulla, and at the end of the war, he was elected consul. Then a new enemy emerged – king Mithridates of Pontus on the Black Sea. Sulla led an army to repel Mithridates' offensive on the Roman province of Asia, but just when the army was to leave, Sulpicius Rufus, a radical tribune, managed to pass a law that shifted the command from Sulla to Marius. Sulla appealed to his men to fight to defend his dignity, and they did. Those men were loyal to him personally, not to the senate, and depended upon him for the properties they had been promised. The Senate had no authority over the warlord with his private army. The Republic's destiny was now in the hands of individuals whose competitive ethos and determination for supremacy could not be limited. The collapse of the Republic had begun.

Chapter 8 – The Age of the Generals: Pompeius, Crassus, and Caesar

The Republic sunk even further after Sulla's death. The shape of Roman history in the following decades was defined by three generals – Gnaeus Pompeius, Marcus Licinius Crassus, and Gaius Julius Caesar. Each of them led an army. They competed for power. Depending on the circumstances they sometimes worked together, sometimes against each other. And they were all brutally killed.

Gnaeus Pompeius

Pompey was born an equestrian, the son of a general. He bravely fought alongside his father in many battles, including the one for Sulla against Marius. His bravery, appearance, and manners granted him enormous popularity. In Africa, where he fought Marius's supporters, he earned the title Magnus (the Great). In Spain, he defeated Sertorius. Maybe the most famous war he participated in was the slave war. From 73 to 71 BC a massive number of slaves from Italy under the gladiator Spartacus revolted. They were well-armed, well-prepared, and not easy to deal with. The general who defeated them was Marcus Licinius Crassus, but Pompey returned from Spain at the very end of the war and claimed all the glory. In 67 BC Pompey crushed the Sicilian pirates in the eastern Mediterranean.

Pompey and Crassus hated each other, but they realized they would be immensely powerful if they worked together. In 70 BC, they became joint consuls. They returned to the tribunes all the authority they had before Sulla's rule. Now they knew they could count on the tribunes in case the Senate tried to make them give up their armies.

In 66 BC, Pompey defeated Mithridates VI, King of Pontus, while he was still around, subjugated Armenia, Syria, and Judaea in 62 BC. Then he did something extraordinary: he established colonies, gave the land to the pirates so they would have something useful to do, and set up a king in Judaea who became his loyal client. Then he returned home and dismissed his army, requiring the Senate to approve his settlement and the land for his veterans. But the only way to achieve this was to join with Crassus and Julius Caesar in the First Triumvirate.

Marcus Licinius Crassus

Crassus was also the son of a general who fought against Marius. He joined Sulla in Italy in 83 BC and was given the reward was to increase his wealth dealing with of Sulla's proscriptions against his enemies. However, Crassus often added innocent people to the list, so he could confiscate their estate. Thus, he lost Sulla's trust but was still popular with the people. Crassus served as praetor, then general, and defeated Spartacus. He hated Pompey for taking the credit but cooperated with him.

Julius Caesar

Gaius Julius Caesar was a Roman aristocrat from the old family of Iulii, which claimed lineage from Aeneas's son Anchises (Iulus). Caesar supported Marius's military control as well as Pompey's restoration of the tribunes. Ambitious and intelligent, he knew how to gain popularity. In 65 BC, in the role of aedile, he spent a lot of public (or Crassus's) wealth on public works and entertainments. In 63 BC he became Pontifex Maximus (the leading priest), by bribing his way to the function. In 62 BC he was mentioned as one of the conspirators, along with Catiline, against the state, but Cicero claimed this was impossible. In 61 BC, Caesar became the governor of Further Spain (present-day Portugal).

The First Triumvirate (60 BC)

The First Triumvirate (the rule of three) was an alliance formed by Pompey, Crassus, and Caesar, who thought they would be even more powerful together. All of them were unsatisfied in their ambitions – Pompey's request for land was blocked by the elite; his mates overshadowed Crassus, and Caesar was not allowed consideration for the consulship in absentia – and they had to do something about it.

Caesar was required to be in Rome in person so that he could be a candidate, so he returned, allied with Pompey and Crassus, and formed the First Triumvirate. Caesar was elected consul in 59 BC. The Senate could not decline the demands of the three generals so easily. Caesar helped Pompey get both the parcels for his soldiers and approval of his reimbursement at the end of the war in the east. Caesar married his daughter Julia to Pompey to fortify their friendship.

Caesar and the Gauls

Caesar became Proconsular Governor in Gaul, which was a position that brought him colossal power. He could still actively participate in Rome's political life, but he also had an army, a significant provincial command with an army, and the possibility of conquest. So, he conquered everything from Rome to the coastlines of the Atlantic and the North Sea. He even led expeditions to Britain, which was believed to be the end of the world.

Caesar himself wrote a detailed account of his nine-year campaign known as the Gallic War. His writing was biased without a doubt – it had to serve him marketing after all – but it contains fantastic detail of this war. Discipline, logistics, quarreling surrounded by the enemy, and the ruthless destruction of risings against Roman rule, he wrote about all of that. Caesar was brutal to the Gauls, to be a Roman hero.

Chapter 9 – Senatus Populus-Que Romanus (SPQR) and Its Downfall

While Caesar was busy fighting in Gaul and Britain and establishing himself as a true Roman Leader, back in Rome, there was a lot of tension. The tribune Publius Clodius Pulcher ("the Handsome") was in control, but his activities endorsed the private interests and competitions that were the trademark of Roman politics. He used Caesar's funds to pay gangs of hooligans to do what they were told. Clodius Pulcher also banished Cicero from Rome using questionable legality of the killings after the supporters. Then he overthrew the king of Cyprus, so he could use his fortune. Next, he imprisoned Pompey in his own home. Pompey reacted with similar measures, employed gangsters, and managed to pass a law which allowed Cicero to return. Pulcher even tried to seduce Caesar's wife, Pompeia. His lewd behavior justified Pompey to increase his authority in Rome at Caesar's expense.

The official name of the Republic at this point was SPQR, meaning the Senate and People of Rome. The title is ironical because the people of Rome had less power than ever before. The care of their interests was handed over to the tribunes, but a tribune could be – and often was – corrupted to his core.

The people of Rome (PQR in SPQR) was a political body made up of all male citizens (the women had no right to vote) of Rome – approximately a million of them in 63 BC. But most of them never turned up in the elections. On the other hand, no one could become a consul unless the people elected him.

Cicero against Catiline: The story that encapsulates 63 BC Rome

Lucius Sergius Catilina (or Catiline) was an angry, bankrupt noble. He was believed to be the architect of a plot to liquidate Rome's elected officials and burn the Senate to the ground. That way, he would write off the debts of rich and poor alike, and debts were again one of the significant problems of populace.

This was one of the central political events of the century. Caesar had some radical ideas about the best way to punish the conspirators. Crassus acted behind the scenes. But the main protagonist and Catalina's opponent was Marcus Tullius Cicero, the renowned orator, politician, philosopher, priest, poet, storyteller, and more. Cicero's name was on the list of those marked out for elimination. This fabulous orator never failed to use his verbal artistry to claim that he had exposed Catiline's awful plan and saved the state. The truth is that this was a turning point in his career, but his finest moment wasn't going to last, nor was the state that he claimed to have saved.

Cicero and Catilina, of course, disagreed politically but was more than the conflict of ideology. Even though they both were at the top of Roman politics, these two men came from different backgrounds. Catilina's family traced its ancestry back to the legendary founding fathers of Rome. They were said to have arrived before Rome even existed. Then there was his great-grandfather fought against Hannibal. Catiline himself was elected to many of junior political offices, but now he was dangerously close to bankruptcy. His name was linked to crimes such as the violent death of his first wife and child and sexual relationship with a "virgin" priestess. But his financial difficulties originated partly from his frequent attempts to buy his way into consulship. He had already been defeated in both

64 and 63 BC, and since the elections were a costly business, he ran out of wealth.

Cicero's story was entirely different. He was a "new man" like Marius. Cicero came from a small town, and no one in his family ever entered the Roman political arena. But he cultivated connections on the highest level and his talent that allowed him to speak his way to the top. He was a brilliant advocate, a superstar, and was elected to junior offices just as easily as Catilina. In 64 BC, Cicero won, Catiline lost. The votes of the wealthy always had more weight, and the Roman elite decided Cicero was a better choice. The second consul elected that year was Gaius Antonius Hybrida, uncle of Marcus Antonius.

In 63 BC, both Cicero and Catiline were candidates again. Cicero acted as he feared his life. He postponed the elections, and when they finally took place, he arrived with an armed guard. A military breastplate was noticeable under his toga. It turned out this tactic worked. Catiline's program worked for Cicero, too, as it further alienated the former patrician from the elite.

Shortly after the elections, Cicero started to receive more proofs of conspiracy from sources such as a certain Fulvia, the girlfriend of one of Catiline's 'collaborators.' Other proofs came with the help of Crassus's money, and Cicero avoided a true assassination attempt in November. Armed forces were grouping outside the city, and Cicero called for the senate to meet and formally condemn and banish Catiline. A decree that allowed Cicero emergency measures to "make sure that the state should come to no harm" had already been issued. Now the senate listened to Cicero's case against Catiline. As always, he was brilliant. His speech was a blend of anger, passion, humility and solid fact. He recapped Catiline's infamous past, expressed heartfelt regret that he had not responded to the threat quickly enough; and revealed details about the conspiracy. Catiline came in person to face the accusation and asked the senators not to trust everything they heard. All he had to say is to insult Cicero's modest background and compare it with his own. But his position was hopeless, and he had to leave the city.

Catiline joined his supporters who had made an army at the border of Rome. In the meantime, Cicero exposed those that were still inside the city. They were arrested, and they tried to act innocent. When the home of one of them was found filled with weapons, he claimed that weapon collecting was his hobby.[xxxiii]

Even though the senate took some time to discuss the destiny of the conspirators, there was never a proper trial. Cicero used his emergency authority, had them all executed, and announced their death in a single word: *vixere*. Literally, it means "they have lived" (but now they are dead).

A few weeks later, Roman legions overpowered Catiline's army in Northen Italy. Catiline fell fighting heroically as a true leader, but the Roman commander, Antonius Hybrida, found an excuse to miss the final battle. Maybe he secretly supported Catiline, and all this hassle had something to do with Crassus. Also, no one knew for sure on which side was Caesar.

Cicero was celebrated as *pater patriae*, one of the finest titles one could have in a society such as Rome. But on his last day as consul, his rivals did not allow him to speak to the people. "Those who have punished others without a hearing ought not to have the right to be heard themselves,"[xxxiv] they said. In 58 BC, the people of Rome voted to banish anyone who had put a citizen to death without trial. Cicero immediately left Rome and spent a year in North Greece. Eventually, the people voted for him to return. His supporters welcomed him warmly, but his house was wiped out and a shrine to Libertas risen instead. He never managed to restore his political career.

Chapter 10 – The Rise and Fall of Julius Caesar and the End of the Roman Republic

The Roman Republic had been declining for years, but finally ended in 43 BC. 15 years later, Rome became the Roman Empire. A single man, Octavian Augustus, modified the regulation of the Republic in a way that he held absolute power.

Caesar versus Pompey

During the First Triumvirate, Crassus, Pompey, and Caesar, each backed by a personal army, forced the Senate to do whatever they required. By 53 BC Crassus was dead, and Caesar and Pompey became rivals – and were yet to become enemies. Both of them had imperium: the power to command an army.

In 50 BC the consul Gaius Marcellus requested Caesar's withdrawal from Gaul. Scribonius Curio, a bankrupt tribune whose support Caesar had bought, vetoed Marcellus's demand, so the consul pleaded Pompey to protect the Republic and use his army and make Caesar surrender his command. Caesar said he would give up his command if Pompey did the same, but this never happened. New governors were sent to the Gallic provinces. The new tribune, Marcus Antonius, tried to veto this decision but was warned he'd soon be dead if he did so. Cicero, even though he was against Caesar and the Triumvirate, wanted to discuss an amicable solution, but the Senate gave Pompey the Senatus Consultum Ultimum, and the power to make Caesar a public enemy and get rid of him once and for all.

Crossing the Rubicon

Caesar had two options available. He could surrender to Rome as a public enemy or stay there and be taken by his adversaries in Gaul. Then he chose the third option: in 49 BC, he took his army from Gaul, crossed the river Rubicon and attacked Italy. This could be a declaration of war against the Republic, but Caesar had nothing to lose. *Iacta alea est*.

Caesar was still willing to share power with Pompey, but the latter was not – or at least his advisors weren't. The war started, Caesar won, and Pompey escaped to Greece.

Caesar seized his city. The senators were frightened, but Caesar's troops were highly disciplined. They didn't ruin anything and did not kill Caesar's opponents. Caesar's reputation was kept intact. Moreover, he made many popular gestures – canceled debts, brought Italians into the Senate, and allowed the men who had been exiled by Sulla and Pompey to return to Rome. Even Pompey's soldiers who remained in Rome were spared and recruited under Caesar.

Caesar sent an army led by Scribonius Curio to Africa, to deal with the rebellion by the governor Attius Varus, who supported Pompey. Curio was defeated. But Caesar almost at the same time went to Pompey's province of Spain and defeated Pompey's two deputies in a month.

Meanwhile, Pompey gathered a vast army in Greece, which included Roman soldiers from border garrisons. He had two times more men than Caesar. Pompey intended to retake Italy, but that didn't work out. The two armies met several times, and Caesar finally beat Pompey at the Battle of Pharsalus in 48 BC. Most of the enemy forces were captured, but Caesar ordered his men to 'spare your fellow citizens.' Pompey escaped to Egypt where he was murdered by the men of the boy-king Ptolemy XIII. When Caesar came for him, he was given his dislodged head. Caesar was angry with Pompey's murders and got them executed.

Ptolemy XIII hoped Caesar would support him against his sister Cleopatra VII. Instead, Caesar placed her to throne by supporting her other brother and husband, Ptolemy XIV. Meanwhile, Cleopatra became his lover and gave birth to his son.

A Romantic Digression: Caesar and Cleopatra

The Egyptian episode deserves a closer look. Some events – not only crucial for the history of the ancient world, but also vital for Caesar's life and career – happened during this visit.

Ptolemy XIII, the ruler of Egypt, depended on Rome's support, maybe even more than other Roman allies at the time. He had no public support whatsoever. His sister and wife (strange as it sounds, but the Egyptian rulers, especially the Ptolemies, loved to keep the power within the family) was the famous Cleopatra VII. She was older and smarter than her brother/husband. People loved her for her generosity and the fact that she was the only person in this ruling dynasty who actually cared about them and spoke Egyptian. She became a queen when she married the legitimate heir to the throne, the aforementioned Ptolemy XIII. He was still a boy at the time – something that enabled Cleopatra to rule alone – but eventually he grew up. He was an entirely different kind of a ruler than she was. Ptolemy XIII was cruel, arrogant, and actually very weak. The people of Egypt hated him, and supported Cleopatra. The ruling couple turned into two of the greatest enemies in the war for the throne of Egypt.

Ptolemy used some dishonest methods to turn the people of Egypt against their beloved queen. His supporters falsified and distributed a decree in her name that all supplies of grain should be sent to Alexandria rather than to the rest of Egypt. As a result, Cleopatra had to abandon the country and find shelter in Syria. But she didn't leave for good. In 48 BC, she gathered an army and came to the border of Egypt, determined to replace Ptolemy on the throne. This was when Caesar stepped in.

Caesar had two reasons to come to Alexandria. He pursued Pompey, but he had also been invited to mediate between Ptolemy and Cleopatra. Ptolemy sent him Pompey's head – an act with vague meaning that could be seen as either a proof of amity or a threat. Caesar was shocked. Pompey was his rival, but Caesar believed he had not deserved such a horrible death. Enraged, Caesar marched into Alexandria and took control over the palace. He ordered both sides to discharge their armies and meet him. Cleopatra knew her husband wouldn't let her enter the city alive. So she entered in disguise, hidden inside an oriental rug, which was delivered to Caesar as a present. Caesar fell in love immediately and that night he and Cleopatra became lovers.

Ptolemy, on the other side, felt betrayed. But he was history. After six months, he was found drowned in the Nile. Cleopatra was almost ready to take the throne. But, as a woman, she was not a legitimate heir. Luckily, her even younger brother Ptolemy XIV was, so she married him. The new Ptolemy was too young for marriage consumption. That pleasure belonged to Caesar. Cleopatra gave birth to his son named Ptolemy Caesar, also known as Caesarion.

Their romantic relationship lasted until Caesar's death. She spent two years in his palace, and was given a number of gifts and titles. After he was murdered, she went back to Egypt, arranged the murder of her husband, and married her son, Caesarion, to make sure he would end up on the throne. That, unfortunately, never happened. After the next episode in her love life – the one that involves Mark Anthony – Octavian Augustus had the young Caesarion executed.

Triumph at Rome

On the way back to Rome in 47 BC, Caesar defeated all opponents from Pharnaces in five days. His victory was summed up in the famous words: *Veni, vidi, vici* (I came, I saw, I conquered). In 46 BC he won the Battle of Thapsus against an army loyal to Pompey.

Caesar became the sole leader of the Roman world. The Senate made Caesar Dictator for ten years. He had to repair the damage, restore the Republic, settle veterans, and reestablish law and order. Caesar brought in concrete solutions to reinstate stability in the Roman world. His reforms included:

- Sparing Pompey's supporters if they were willing to come over to Caesar.
- Reducing the number of idle troublemakers by halving the number of Romans who depended on the free corn dole.
- Settling his army veterans in foreign colonies.
- Setting up new colonies and giving them Roman or at least Latin status.
- Granting Roman citizenship to those who deserved it.
- Permitting Italians, and some Gauls, to the Senate, and extending the Senate's awareness of issues outside Rome.
- Upgrading road links to the port at Ostia.
- Granting Latin status to Transpadane Gaul.
- Reducing taxes in some provinces.

Caesar was admired for his reforms. He indeed had done a lot to assure stability in the Roman world. The Senate thought Caesar would operate within the Republican system, but this wasn't the case. He still had his powerful army. Moreover, he appointed himself a consul several years and took over the powers of a tribune. Traditionalists criticized him for suppressing the Republican system. He filled the Senate with his men and did whatever he wanted. His word was law. Caesar crossed the line several times, and one of his mistakes was that he allowed statues of himself along with those of gods and the kings. His coins had his portrait. Everything he did annoyed his quiet opponents. In 44 BC, Caesar became Dictator Perpetuus (Dictator for Life) and acted like a king.

The Roman people only cared about stability and leadership; they were happy because Caesar's reforms put an end to the years of struggle. But senators resented him, and Cicero called him a tyrant. Caesar thought he was invincible and did not have a bodyguard anymore. He was preparing to defeat Parthia, fulfill a prophecy and become a Roman king.

Caesar's adversaries knew he would leave on 18 March 44 BC if they didn't do something immediately. On March 15, 44 BC, the Ides of Brutus and Cassius stabbed him at a Senate meeting. They thought they had liberated Rome from a tyrant and would be celebrated as the liberators of the Republic, but they were wrong. Brutus and other conspirators found the empty Forum. The senators left, and so did everybody else. The conspirators knew they should leave the town.

Mark Antony took charge. He was Caesar's co-consul and loyal supporter over many years. Cicero – who was one of the conspirators - believed Antony should have been eliminated too.

Caesar's funeral triggered public rage. The crowd vandalized the Forum and lynched someone who looked like one of the conspirators. A group of men hurried toward Brutus' and Cassius's homes to kill them, but they had escaped and fled Rome.

Mark Antony or Octavian

Mark Antony managed to calm people and stabilize a possibly catastrophic situation after Caesar's assassination. He intentionally let the conspirators to get away, gave some land away from Rome to Caesar's veterans, and ended the dictatorship. Brutus and Cassius even became governors of provinces. But the Senate did not approve of the way Antony was spending funds and selling benefits using bogus documents. Finally, the Senate named someone else as

Caesar's heir – his great-nephew and adopted son, Gaius Octavius Thurinus, who became known as Octavianus. Octavian was a legitimate heir, according to Caesar's will.

The End of the Republic (44–43 BC)

The 18-year-old Octavian promptly arrived from Epirus, where he attended military training, to Rome, changing his name to Gaius Julius Caesar Octavianus, to make sure he would win over Caesar's troops. The tension between himself and Marc Antony, who was carelessly spending Caesar's fortune, started right away. Cicero also criticized Antony for his opportunism.

Antony became governor in Gaul and intended to move the army from Macedonia into Gaul. He was planning to attack Brutus, and the Senate declared him a public enemy.

The Senate wanted Octavian to become an ally of Brutus and punished him by holding up the money when they didn't want to do so. At last, Octavian met Antony, and together with Marcus Aemilius Lepidus, the Governor of Spain, they formed the Second Triumvirate, which lasted for five years. The power of the Second Triumvirate diminished the one of the Senate. Octavian, Antony, and Lepidus could do whatever they wanted. The law that established the Second Triumvirate was passed on 27 November 43 BC. It was the end of the Roman Republic. Just a decade later, Octavian would become the undisputed master of the Roman Empire.

Conclusion

The rise and decline of the Roman Republic have a distinctive place in the history of the Western world. From modest beginnings on seven hills alongside the River Tiber, the city of Rome became the dominant power in the ancient Mediterranean world. Led by the senatorial nobles, Republican military forces triumphed over Carthage and the successor monarchies to Alexander the Great and took the nearby cities and tribes to east and west under Roman rule. However, the accomplishment of the Republic was also a seed of catastrophe. The same forces that propelled the growth and conquests of Rome, and the treasures that conquests brought, caused political, social, and economic crisis and rushed the Republic into the chaos of civil war. The Senate and other Republican institutions couldn't cope with the weights of sustaining Rome's empire, and at the end, all power came into the hands of Octavianus Augustus, the first Roman emperor.

For the generations yet to come, the Roman Republic has offered a pattern, inspiration, and a warning. The legends of the Roman past and the heroes and enemies of the Republic have never stopped rousing the imagination. Books, films, and series still rely on that legacy today, even though their level of historical accuracy is far from perfect. The Republic's history itself is as fascinating as any fiction. It consists of moments of highest drama, from the mythical story of Romulus, Hannibal's journey over the Alps to Julius Caesar on the shores of the Rubicon and in the Senate on the Ides of March.

Two thousand years have passed since the Roman Republic fell, but its legacy is still alive. The Roman Empire which arose from the ashes of the Republic continued to rely on Republican traditions, even as imperial tyranny took the place of joint senatorial rule. The slow transformation of the Empire to Christianity added a new element, with admiration for Rome's antiquity combined with criticism of its pagan past.

Over the next couple of centuries, the influence of the Roman Republic faded, until the Renaissance. The political theory of Machiavelli and Shakespeare's plays helped revive the ideals, heroes, and anti-heroes of Republican history. This new awareness of the Roman past had more significant consequences in the 18th century when the great revolutions in France and America found inspiration in the notions of a Republican utopia. The Roman Republic still spreads through modern Western culture from politics to popular culture, influencing our lives so many ways.

Timeline[xxxv]

All dates are B.C.

754/3 Traditional date of Rome's foundation

509 Expulsion of the Etruscan kings; the foundation of the Republic

494 First tribunes of the plebs elected

451/450 Law of the Twelve Tables

396 Capture of Veii

390/386 Gauls sack Rome

367 Licinio-Sextian laws: sharing of political power between the patricians and plebeians

282—275 War with Pyrrhus, king of Epirus

264 First gladiatorial combat in Rome

264—241 First Punic War

241 Sicily becomes the first Roman province

238 Provinces of Sardinia and Corsica established

225 Gauls invade Italy

219/218 Lex Claudia limits commercial activities of senators

218—201 Second Punic War

200—146 Wars against Macedonia and in the East

197 Two Spanish provinces established; Philip V, king of Macedonia, defeated at Cynoscephalae

196 Flamininus proclaims Greece's freedom 190 Antiochus III, king of Syria, defeated at Magnesia

186 Suppression of the Bacchanalian cult in Italy

168 Perseus, king of Macedonia, defeated at Pydna

149 First permanent jury court established

149-146 Third Punic War

146 Destruction of Corinth and Carthage; provinces of Macedonia and Africa established

133 Pergamum bequeathed to Rome by its last king, Attalus III

133—12 Reforms of the Gracchi brothers

129 Province of Asia established

121 Province of Gallia Narbonensis (Provence) established; first suspension of the constitution

112—105 War with Jugurtha, king of Numidia

107 Marius' army reforms

100 Province of Cilicia established

91—87 Social War: all Italians become Roman citizens; Sulla captures Rome

83-82 Civil war

82 Sulla captures Rome

82—79 Sulla controls Rome: restoration of the Republic

75/74 Province of Cyrenaica established

67 Province of Crete established; defeat of pirates

66—63 Pompey in the East

64 Province of Syria established 63 Province of Bithynia and Pontus established; consulship of Cicero; Catilinarian conspiracy

60 Political alliance of Pompey, Caesar, and Crassus

59 Province of Cyprus and province of IUyricum established; consulship of Caesar

58—50 Gallic War 49 Caesar crosses the Rubicon and invades Italy

49—45 Civil war between Caesar and his senatorial opponents (esp. Pompey and Cato)

44 Caesar is named dictator for life; Caesar is assassinated on the Ides of March

43 Triumvirate consisting of Antony, Octavian, and Lepidus; the assassination of Cicero

42 Brutus and Cassius die after defeat at Philippi

31 Battle of Actium: Octavian defeats Antony and Cleopatra

27 Octavian "restores the Republic" and takes the name Augustus

Preview of Ancient Greece
A Captivating Guide to Greek History Starting from the Greek Dark Ages to the End of Antiquity

Introduction

The period commonly referred to as Ancient Greece spans a broad scope of time from the Grecian Dark Ages in approximately 1100 BC to the End of Antiquity in around AD 600. Just as the time is extensive in range, so was the geography of Greece. Over that period, in fact, the borders sometimes grew to encompass many other modern-day regions. At other times, the boundaries shrank, and for a period the region was under the dominion of the Roman Empire. Even still, the reach of Greece was strong, with neighbouring areas being profoundly influenced by Greek culture and events.

The culture and events of Greece were so influential they have a significant effect on modern-day people all over the world. The ancient Greeks gave birth to democracy, a political system frequently used and considered by some as the best form of government. Great minds from Greece also made incredible and vital discoveries such as the water mill, the basics of geometry and using medicine to cure illness. The ancient Greek philosophers laid the groundwork for a whole new field of thought and study. Ancient Greece offered the foundation of the Olympic games, which still run regularly today. Particularly famous historical figures such as Alexander the Great and Cleopatra also had ties to and roles during Greek history, through the course of wars and empire expansion.

Given the influence of Ancient Greece, as you learn about this time and place, you will learn about your history and the origins of the people, places, and institutions you likely regularly studied in school. Starting in the Dark Ages, it is quite a journey through the darkness, democracy, discovery, and development of Western Civilization.

Chapter 1 – Dawn of the Dark Ages

For approximately 500 years, the Mycenaean civilization resided in the geographic area now known as Greece. In about 1200 BC, the Mycenaean civilization started to collapse. Archaeological records suggest that by around 1100 BC, the cities, outlying settlements, and the entire organization of the Mycenaeans' culture began to be abandoned or destroyed. By 1050 BC, the recognizable features of Mycenaean culture had nearly entirely disappeared, and the population was significantly reduced. Many historians provide explanations for the cause of this downturn. Some attribute the fall of the Mycenaean civilization, which coincided with the collapse the Bronze Age, to climatic or environmental catastrophe. Others attribute it to invasion by the Dorians or the "Sea Peoples." No single explanation fits all the available archaeological evidence.

Invasions by a group known as the "Sea Peoples" may have contributed to the collapse of the Mycenaean civilization. Their exact origins remain a mystery. The "Sea Peoples" may have come from as far away as the northern shores of the Black Sea, or from as close nearby as the Aegean Sea or from along the Mediterranean coasts of Asia Minor. The Egyptians named these peoples, in inscriptions and carvings at Karnak and Luxor. The Egyptians had some initial military successes against these foreign warriors. However, even Egypt could not escape the repercussions of these attacks, which spanned the entirety of the Eastern Mediterranean, subsuming the area of modern-day Greece, and leading to the dawn of the Dark Ages.

The collapse of Mycenaean civilization caused significant disruptions to people's way of life in the region. There was economic hardship, famine, and political instability. Large-scale revolts took place, and powerful kingdoms were wholly overthrown. Crucial trade connections were lost. Towns and villages were abandoned or burned to the ground. The population of Greece was reduced, perhaps by half, and whole systems of organization ceased: state armies, kings, administrators, and trade connections disappeared.

Due to the collapse of large cities, great planned construction projects and wall painting for the arts could not continue to completion. The use of the Linear B writing system ceased. This reduced the ability for record keeping and therefore information on this period in Greek history comes only from the remains and artifacts found in burial sites.

The fragmented societies that remained were mostly isolated from one another, and thus each developed their own cultures, pottery styles, burial practices, and other settlement features. Again, records are almost non-existent, but pottery has been found in archaeological sites. The pottery style, which is known as Proto-Geometric, was substantially less complex than designs that existed before the collapse. This is a sign that progress in development had been lost and in some cases, even regressed.

It is likely that during this period, the divisions of the region were organized by kinship groups and the oikoi (or households). This style laid the origins of the later poleis (political nature of Greece). Due to the disparate societies, generalizations about a more extensive community cannot be made. The various people throughout the region that survived the initial collapse cannot be grouped in any meaningful way because they spent too much time disconnected from each other. Some areas in Greece, such as Attica, Euboea, and central Crete, recovered their economy faster than others.

Luckily, not all was lost for the future of the region. There were still some advances during this time. They were just limited and slower in progress than they may have otherwise been. There was still farming, weaving, metalworking, and pottery, but at a much lower level of output and only for local consumption. There was some limited technical progress, such as a faster potter's wheel and the development of the compass (for the drawing of geometric patterns). Longer lasting glazes were also developed by higher firing temperature.

Perhaps most importantly and influential for the ongoing history of the region, methods for smelting iron came from Cyprus and the Levant, and drew upon local sources of iron ore. Iron weapons were now within reach of less elite warriors, and the universal adoption of iron was a critical feature for most Dark Age settlements. From 1050 onward, several local iron industries appeared, and by 900, almost all graves contained at least some iron implements.

With time and work, some communities were able to return from their setbacks. Archaeologists can study these communities to better understand their structure and the timing of events. For example, excavations of Dark Age communities such as Nicosia in the Peloponnese have demonstrated how a Bronze Age town was abandoned in 1150 but then re-emerged as a small cluster of villages by 1075.

At that time, only around 40 families were living there with plenty of good farming land and grazing for cattle. The remains of a 10th-century building, including a megaron (great hall typical of Greek palaces), on the top of the ridge, have led to speculation this was the leader's house or a place of religious significance. This was a larger structure than those surrounding it, but it was still made from the same materials (mud brick and thatched roof).

High-status individuals did, in fact, exist in the Dark Ages, but their standard of living was not significantly higher than others in their village. Most Greeks did not live in isolated farmsteads because living far from organized societies increased the danger and risk of being attacked by enemies. Instead, they lived in small settlements. It is likely that for the next two to three hundred years, the primary economic source for most families was through farming on their ancestral plot of land.

The archaeological records show that by the start of the 8th century BC, several sites in Greece saw robust economic recovery. Long distance trade was re-established, by connecting the Near East, Greece, Egypt, and Italy. Archaeological findings show Greek pottery in northern Syria and among the Villanovan culture in Italy, which shows evidence for those trade routes.

As time passed, the forms, styles, and decoration of pottery became more complex and included figurative scenes that appear to come from the Homeric Epics *The Iliad* and *The Odyssey*. This showed that attention to the arts had re-emerged. Iron tools and weapons also continued to develop and increased in quality.

Mediterranean trade brought new supplies of copper and tin to the region of Greece from distant places. This allowed artisans to craft a wide variety of elaborate bronze tools and items. Other coastal regions of Greece were once again becoming full participants in the commercial and cultural exchanges of the eastern and central Mediterranean. Simultaneously, local governance increased in complexity, changing from single-leader autocracies to oligarchies or other forms of aristocratic rulership.

Although the region of Greece had faced its Dark Ages, which brought setbacks to their way of life. The people re-built all that was lost. As methods for government started to evolve there, the region moved from the Dark ages into the enlightenment of Democracy.

Chapter 2 – From Darkness to Democracy

As the region of Greece moved away from the demand for mere survival brought about by the Dark Ages, the people could think about living well. The existing state organization, government, and political leadership had been comprised of many separate, but equal groups. Luckily, the Grecian people saw a better solution than just infighting for power. They envisioned a solution for governance that would allow all people to be considered equally. It was a revolutionary approach, and one many countries use today—Democracy.

The development of Democracy among the Greek city-states was slow, yet continually developing process. Democracy in Athens grew in fits and starts, but eventually, it blossomed to its fullest extent. Its humble beginnings began with the politician Solon.

In the period before Solon's leadership, most of the city-states had tyrannical (rule by a single person), aristocratic, or oligarchic governments. Then, in 632 BC, following the misinterpreted advice of an oracle, a nobleman named Cylon, attempted a coup in Athens. The coup failed with Cylon, his brother, and other followers seeking refuge in the Temple of Athena. Cylon and his brother eventually escaped. The attempted coup resulted in a period of shifting alliances and economic stagnation in Athens.

In approximately 593 BC, due to the political climate of the time, Solon was given almost unlimited power when he was elected to the office of Archon. Solon decided to write dictates designed to solve the political problems plaguing the city. Solon's dictates were inscribed on wooden plaques that were hung up for the citizens to read. Solon repealed all the laws (except those concerning homicide).

Before Solon's reforms, Athens was administered by nine Archons, who were elected or appointed. There was also an assembly of commoners (the *ekklesia*). However, there was no representative body for the lowest class of citizens (the Thetes). Solon altered the rules for the *ekklesia*, allowing all male citizens to be allowed into it, with court magistrates and juries drawn from the same pool of males. This could be considered as an early version of the Republic form of government, in which citizens have a role in the creation of laws and the means to hold elected leaders accountable.

To guide such a large governing body, Solon also created the Council of Four Hundred. For this, each of the four Athenian tribes put forward one hundred members to serve on the Council. Solon also made alterations to the organization of Athens' military by stratifying the roles and delineating who could serve in them according to their family wealth or property.

Solon also reformed the economic laws and culture of Athens. Fathers were encouraged to find trades or suitable economic roles for their sons. Otherwise, the sons would not be required to support their fathers in old age. Foreign craftsmen and merchants were encouraged to move to Athens with their families and were granted citizenship. The cultivation of olives and the production of olive-based products was supported, and the export of all other produce was prohibited. Solon also propagated laws regarding some forms of slavery: annulling all contracts based on personal servitude, banning debt-based slavery, and releasing all Athenian citizens from all forms of slavery. Furthermore, Solon also passed several other social reforms to improve Athenian life.

Once his rules were disseminated, and he saw they were working, Solon left Athens for ten years, travelling the various territories of the Eastern Mediterranean. The reforms did not last long, however, as the old ways were challenging to give up. Within four years, some elected officials refused to stand down once their terms were up, while other important posts sometimes remained empty. Eventually, a relative of Solon, Peisistratus, seized power as a tyrant ruling over Athens. Upon returning after his ten years, Solon regarded the Athenians as foolish for allowing this to happen.

After Peisistratus died in 527 BC, his son, Hippias, became a tyrant. Hippias was cruel to the citizens of Athens. He levied crushing taxes on the poor and executed large numbers of people. This caused immense hostility towards his rule, and he began looking abroad for allies, first in Persia and then in Lampsakos. Other Athenian families, concerned about any relationship with Persia, sought to overthrow Hippias. Eventually, he was ousted by a Spartan military campaign in 510 BC and banished from Athens along with his family. Hippias and his family joined the Achaemenid Empire.

Following the expulsion of Hippias, democracy was brought back through the reforms of Cleisthenes, during 508 BC. His first change altered the political boundaries of Athens, broadening them to contain the entire region of Attica, and regarding all the free people there as citizens. Further changes were made in 462 BC by Ephialtes, which significantly reduced the power of the existing leadership body, turning it solely into a court for the trying of deliberate homicide. In the fourth century BC, the leadership body was again modified, adding responsibility for investigating corruption among officials.

By the fourth century BC, Athenian democracy had reached its maturity. Like today, some Athenians were more politically active or ambitious than others. The governing bodies of the city were complex, multi-faceted, and involved a 'checks-and-balances' system to ensure stability. To vote, one had to be an adult, male citizen. Aside from participation in politics, being male certainly gave ancient Grecians many more rights and abilities. Something that was also demonstrated in the ancient Olympic games.

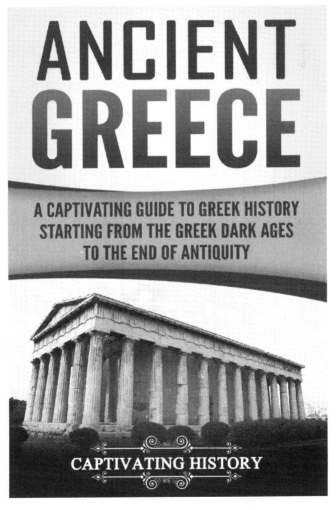

Check out this book!

Preview of Maya Civilization

A Captivating Guide to Maya History and Maya Mythology

Introduction

You've probably heard of the Maya and their astounding civilization before. You may recognize the famous Maya calendar that apparently predicted a worldwide apocalypse back in 2012. The media were quick to jump on board this mind-boggling prophecy (which we'll debunk later in this book). Newspapers and websites were filled with stories of doomsday that failed to materialize. Lucky for us, we did wake up on December 22, 2012, when the Maya calendar apparently ended.

But what you may not know is how much the Maya legacy is impacting your life today. Do you love to treat yourself to a frothy hot chocolate before bed, or indulge in an after-dinner chocolate treat? Do you love adding a side of fries to your meal? What about tomatoes for your favorite Italian dishes? If you do, you may not be aware that you have the Maya and the Spanish conquistadors to thank, for they introduced these goods to Europe and other continents.

But Maya are far more than just their food. In this captivating guide, you'll discover why Maya have gained such worldwide admiration over the many other civilizations that existed in Mesoamerica at the time. You'll learn how the Maya civilization developed, the major turning points in their 3,000-year-long history, the mysteries surrounding their demise, and some of the unique places where Maya exist to this day.

Oh yes. If you think the Maya are gone, think again. As opposed to popular belief, the Maya are neither extinct, nor quiet. They are six-million strong, according to some sources, most of them living in Guatemala. What's more, in 1994 one of the surviving Maya tribes, the Zapatistas, launched a rebellion in southeast Mexico against global trade and capitalism.

In the first part of this book, we'll first examine the origins of the Maya civilization and the Mesoamerican cultures that may have influenced them. We'll discuss why Maya (out of all the different tribes that existed in the region at the time) have captured the imagination of the West so much. We'll look at how they lived, ate, slept, whom they worshipped, and how they used herbal medicines and hallucinogenic plants to treat the sick.

We'll look at their trading routes and rivalries with another famous Mesoamerican tribe—the Aztecs. We'll look into the decline of the Maya civilization and how their rivalries with the Aztecs aided the victory of the Spanish conquistadors in the 16th century, led by the famous Spaniard Hernán Cortés. We won't forget to mention the heroic efforts of the Maya to fend off the Spaniards, and why they were able to succeed at this task for much longer than the Aztecs. We'll even track down the Maya living today, a population that is still six-million strong and adhere to many of the traditions that their ancestors once held. In among the battle tales and gore of human sacrifice, we'll look at some delicious cocoa recipes, Maya-style, that you can make at home.

After we've learnt all about the Maya origins, their cuisine, and their most notable events to present day, we'll delve into the aspect that's often the reason why so many people have been fascinated by the Maya civilization throughout the ages. We will look at their mythology, cosmology, and the solar calendar that resulted in the infamous doomsday scare back in 2012.

So buckle up and get ready to be transported to the warm and wet plains of the Maya civilization—it will be a journey you'll never forget.

Maya Timeline

The Archaic Period:
- 7000 to 2000 BC

The Preclassic Period:
- Early Preclassic – 2000 to 1000 BC
- Middle Preclassic – 1000 to 300 BC
- Late Preclassic – 300 BC to AD 250

The Classic Period:
- Early Classic – AD 250 to 600
- Late Classic – AD 600 to 900
- Terminal Classic – AD 900 to 1000

The Postclassic Period:
- Early Postclassic – AD 1000 to 1250
- Late Postclassic – AD 1250 to 1521
- The Spanish Invasion – AD 1521

Glossary of Important Maya Terms
- Cacao – the seeds that the Maya used in order to create their delicious cacao drink, also known as "bitter water."
- Cenote – a type of sink-hole that the Maya used to get fresh supplies of water (and to perform ritual sacrifice).
- Conquistadors – the Spanish military leaders who led the conquest of America in the 16th century, including Hernándo Cortés.
- The Dresden Codex – located in a museum in Germany, the Dresden Codex is one of the oldest surviving books from the

Americas. It contains 78 pages with important information on rituals, calculations, and the planetary movements of Venus.
- Haab – one of the several Maya calendars (this one measured time in 365-day cycles).
- Hero Twins – the central characters in the Maya creation story and the ancestors of future Maya rulers.
- Huipil – traditional dress for Maya women.
- Maize – the staple food of Maya civilization, an ancient form of corn (the Maize god was one of the most important deities for Maya).
- Mesoamerica – this is what we call the region of the Americas before the arrival of the Spanish fleets and its colonisation in the 15th and 16th centuries.
- Popol Vuh – the story of creation of the world that was passed down from generation to generation (it was recorded by the Quiche Maya who lived in the region of modern day Guatemala).
- Shamanism – an important spiritual practice throughout Mesoamerica (during shamanic trance a shaman would be able to practice divination and healing).
- Stelae – an upright stone slab or column, often used as a gravestone. These structures usually contained commemorative inscriptions.
- Yucatan Peninsula – a region in the southeast of Mexico, where some of the Maya civilization developed, especially in the Postclassic period.

Part 1 – History

Chapter 1: The Origins of the Mesoamerican Civilizations

Maya have captivated the imagination of the West ever since their culture was "discovered" in the 1840s by the American writer and explorer John Lloyd Stephens and the English artist and architect Frederick Catherwood. The latter is best known for his intricate and detailed images of the Maya ruins that he and Stephens later published in their book *Incidents of Travel in Central America*.

But just because the West didn't discover the Maya until the mid-nineteenth century doesn't mean that they lived in obscurity the rest of the time. In fact, their history is rich with fantastical tales and splendour and a diet that people living in other regions at the time could only dream about. The origins of the Maya civilization can be traced all the way back to 7,000 BC.

The Archaic period: 7000 – 2000 BC

People were once hunter-gatherers, living a largely nomadic lifestyle, according to the whims of nature and the sharp-toothed animals all around them. They had to keep moving in order to stay safe and keep up their food supplies. But in 7000 BC a new shift began—the hunter-gatherers who lived in Mesoamerica discovered something that would change their region forever. They began planting crops.

It's not entirely clear why this shift occurred when it did. The changing weather patterns may have had something to do with it—the climate gradually became wetter and warmer, so many of the larger animals that the Mesoamericans relied on for food became extinct. As a result, they had to eat more plants and grains, so eventually they started growing some for themselves. They used many techniques to make their lands more fertile. For example, they discovered that burning trees helped put nitrates into the soil to make it more fertile. (Don't try this at home.)

As a result, these ancient people started having a much more varied diet. We know this thanks to the discoveries by the archaeologists working in the Tehuacan Valley of Mexico, a site that contains the best evidence for human activity in the Archaic time period in Mesoamerica. The locals were able to plant and eat things that we often take for granted today, such as peppers, squash, and avocado. Not to mention early forms of corn, the grain that would become the staple food in Mesoamerica.

Since they were able to grow the food that they needed in order to survive, these ancient people no longer needed to move around as much. They began settling down into small villages, leading to the first known settlements in Mesoamerica. The first evidence of individual burial spots directly under people's homes dates back to 2600 BC. These early settlements included temples and sacred spots for worship, suggesting an early form of a civilization. Temples, worship, and sacrifice remained a prominent theme throughout the Maya history, and we'll cover more of it later.

But the Maya did not evolve in a vacuum. There were many cultures and tribes that existed around them, and each had some influence on their culture, customs, and civilization. We'll examine these, one at a time, as we travel through time to really appreciate the interplay between those cultures and the Maya. Before we go onto learning about how these early settlements evolved into the Maya civilization, let's look at one of the most important tribes that existed in Mesoamerica at the time—the Olmecs.

The Olmecs: 1,200 – 300 BC

No one really knows where the Olmecs came from or where they disappeared to. But their legacy on the Mesoamerican tribes, including the Maya, is huge.

The Olmecs inhabited the area along the Gulf of Mexico, and their impressive stone cities gave way to myths about giants who may have lived in this area at the time. The Olmec craftsmanship was highly sophisticated—there are some impressive sculptures that survive to this day as evidence of their superb skills.

Sometimes ancient history is a bit of guesswork, leaving you to fill in the gaps left out by missing evidence. It's interesting that there's a total lack of battle scenes in the Olmec art—something that most other cultures are quick to display in their monuments and sculptures. The fact that they depict no battle scenes could mean one of two things. Either they did not engage in any war conflict, or they simply didn't feel like showing off about it. You decide.

Until recently, the Olmecs were regarded as the "mother culture" of all the great Mesoamerican civilizations to come, including the Maya and the Aztecs. But more recent sources argue that the Maya actually had a counter-influence on the Olmecs.

When it comes to the Olmec mythology, displayed in their surviving temples and sculptures, there are definite traces of shamanic practice. Many of their sculptures depict a were-jaguar, a core element of shamanism, symbolizing shamanic trance. The Maya saw the jaguar as a transformational animal, who feels at home at night-time, a symbol for the Underworld. The symbolism of shamanistic practice is present in all later Mesoamerican cultures, including the Maya.

The Olmecs may have had an important motif of a twin deity, that may have influenced the mythology of the Maya Hero Twins. The Hero Twins is a way to express the duality that the Maya saw around them—the complementary duality between day and night, life and death, the masculine and the feminine. The Olmec flaming eyebrows, the first corn, and cross bands are all symbols that would later appear in the Maya art, connected to astrology. Ancestor worship was also prevalent in the Olmec tradition, as it was later in the Maya and most Mesoamerican cultures at the time.

Challenge your perceptions—Dwarfism

When studying ancient history and learning about cultures, it's always interesting to find out what light it can shed on the culture that we inhabit today. Sometimes the things that we perceive as true are to do with our cultural upbringing. For example, nowadays we define people who are born with smaller organisms and don't grow much taller than 147cm as having the medical condition of Dwarfism or "short stature." We tend to see this as an abnormality, assuming that people born with this condition would face certain limitations in life.

Well, the Olmec also saw Dwarfism as an abnormality, only not a limiting one. In fact, it was quite the opposite. As the director of the Maya Exploration Center, Dr. Edwin Barnhart explains in his audio-lecture series *Maya To Aztec: Ancient Mesoamerica Revealed* that if you were born with a very small organism in the Olmec or the later Maya culture, you'd be seen as a magical being, touched by the gods. You'd be enjoying all kinds of luxuries, often appearing in the king's court. This may be something to do with their belief that the sky was held up by four dwarves, and so they gave them special treatment.

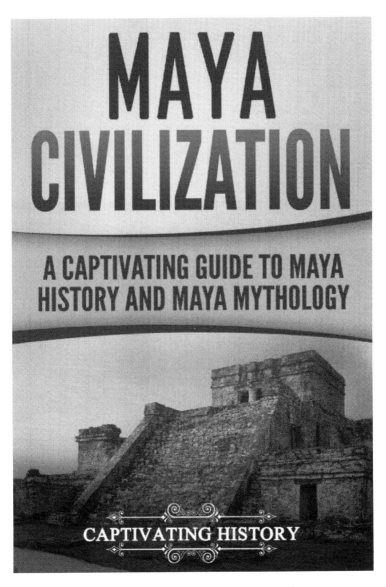

Check out this book!

References

[i] Harriet I. Flower, *The Cambridge Companion to the Roman Republic*, Cambridge University Press, 2006
[ii] Mary Beard, *SPQR: A History of Ancient Rome*, Profile Books, London, 2015
[iii] The word 'candidate' derives from the Latin candidatus, which means 'whitened' and refers to the specially whitened togas that Romans wore during election campaigns, to impress the voters. (Beard)
[iv] A letter to Atticus
[v] Titus Livius (59 BC – 17 AD) was a Roman historian. His history of Rome from its foundation to his own time contained 142 books, of which 35 survive.
[vi] As referred by Beard (*SPQR, A History of Ancient Rome*)
[vii] According to Livy
[viii] Publius Ovidius Naso, *The Art of Love (Ars Amatoria)*, Book One, available online at: **https://en.wikisource.org/wiki/Ars_Amatoria:_The_Art_of_Love/1**
[ix] *The Guardian*, "Ovid's exile to the remotest margins of the Roman empire revoked" https://www.theguardian.com/world/2017/dec/16/ovids-exile-to-the-remotest-margins-of-the-roman-empire-revoked
[x] David M. Gwynn, *The Roman Republic: A Very Short Introduction,* Oxford University Press; 2012
[xi] Plutarch, *Moralia, On the fortune of the Romans* http://www.gutenberg.org/ebooks/23639
[xii] Livy; also: T. P. Wiseman, *Remus: A Roman Myth*. New York: Cambridge University Press, 1995
[xiii] Painting by Jean Bardin, 1765. https://upload.wikimedia.org/wikipedia/commons/d/d5/Bardin_Tullia.jpg
[xiv] Beard, as above
[xv] Beard
[xvi] Gwynn, as above
[xvii] Stephen P. Oakley, "The Early Republic," *The Cambridge Companion to the Roman Republic*, edited by Harriet I. Flower, Cambridge University Press, 2006
[xviii] Gwynn
[xix] Oakley, as above
[xx] Livy
[xxi] The word 'dictator' in ancient Rome had a different meaning than it has in modern world. It was a military title, not a synonym for a 'tyrant.'
[xxii] Michael Grant, *History of Rome*, Faber, 1979
[xxiii] These were the same walls that were said to have been built by Servius Tullius

and are still known as the "Servian Walls"
[xxiv] Alexander the Great's brother-in-law
[xxv] Polybius was a pro-Roman Greek historian from Megalopolis
[xxvi] Gwynn
[xxvii] Livy
[xxviii] Livy
[xxix] Gwynn
[xxx] Plutarch, *Life of Flamininus*
[xxxi] "Greece, the captive, made her savage victor captive, and brought the arts into rustic Latium." Horace, Epistles 2.1.156, in Horace: *Satires, Epistles, and Ars Poetica*
[xxxii] Polybius, Histories
[xxxiii] Beard
[xxxiv] Cited according to Beard; the exact source unknown
[xxxv] The Cambridge Companion to the Roman Republic Cambridge University Press, 2006

Free Bonus from Captivating History (Available for a Limited time)

Hi History Lovers!

Now you have a chance to join our exclusive history list so you can get your first history ebook for free as well as discounts and a potential to get more history books for free! Simply visit the link below to join.

Captivatinghistory.com/ebook

Also, make sure to follow us on:

Twitter: @Captivhistory

Facebook: Captivating History: @captivatinghistory

ABOUT CAPTIVATING HISTORY

A lot of history books just contain dry facts that will eventually bore the reader. That's why Captivating History was created. Now you can enjoy history books that will mesmerize you. But be careful though, hours can fly by, and before you know it; you're up reading way past bedtime.

Get your first history book for free here:
http://www.captivatinghistory.com/ebook

Make sure to follow us on Twitter: @CaptivHistory and Facebook: www.facebook.com/captivatinghistory so you can get all of our updates!

Made in the USA
Middletown, DE
17 September 2018